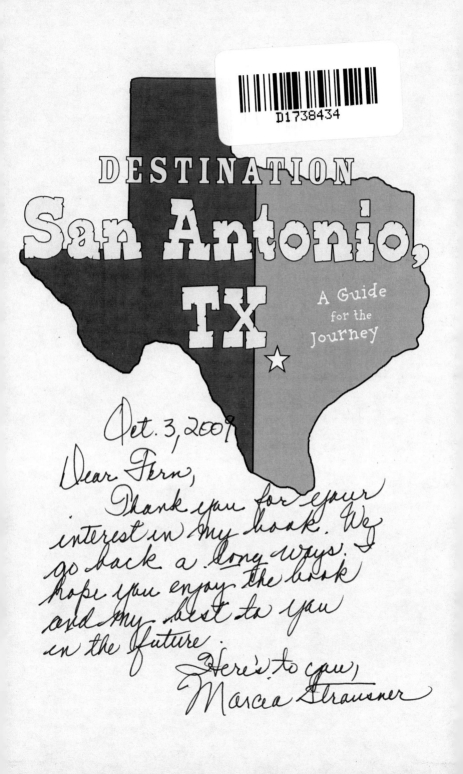

DESTINATION
San Antonio,
TX

A Guide
for the
Journey

Oct. 3, 2009

Dear Fern,

Thank you for your
interest in my book. We
go back a long ways. I
hope you enjoy the book
and my best to you
in the future.

Here's to you,
Marcia Strausner

DESTINATION
San Antonio, TX

A Guide
for the
Journey

written by
Marcia Strausner

TATE PUBLISHING
& Enterprises

Published by Tate Publishing & Enterprises, LLC
127 E. Trade Center Terrace | Mustang, Oklahoma 73064 USA
1.888.361.9473 | www.tatepublishing.com

Tate Publishing is committed to excellence in the publishing industry. The company reflects the philosophy established by the founders, based on Psalm 68:11,
"The Lord gave the word and great was the company of those who published it."

Book design copyright © 2009 by Tate Publishing, LLC. All rights reserved.
Cover and Interior design by Eddie Russell
Illustration by Katie Brooks

Published in the United States of America

ISBN: 978-1-60696-640-2
Juvenile Fiction: Historical: United States: General
09.03.25

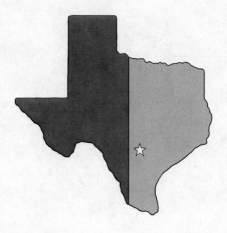

This book is dedicated to my grandchildren, Anna, Daniel, Ryan, and Brady and to all my former students at Verda James Elementary School in Casper, Wyoming.

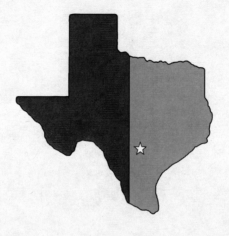

Acknowledgments

It is exciting to write a first book! However, it takes determination, a strong will to initiate the process, courage to believe in oneself, perseverance in completing the manuscript, and strong support from family, friends, and colleagues. Support comes in many forms. It comes with the willingness of friends and family to share the writer's time with the writing process. It comes with the willingness to become an editor and knowing how to tactfully offer suggestions. Support and encouragement also come by expressing interest in the progress of the manuscript and, when completed, interest in the publishing and marketing of the book. My husband, LeRoy; daughters, Gaye and Rachelle; and their husbands, Mark and Keith, have shown this support. Sue Heisner, my friend and the librarian at Verda James Elementary School, acted as my editor and confidant. Alberta Giraldo was my very competent Spanish translator. I also want to acknowledge God as my muse and to honor my students, teacher friends, and family members whose names I have used in the book. You all inspired me, and I have stored your stories in my head and have treasured you in my heart. Thank you. Thank you.

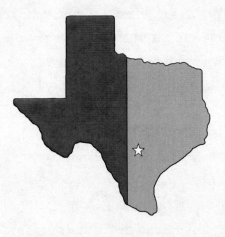

Contents

Why Siblings Spy

Anna had just said goodnight to God. Like
the goodnight hug from her parents, her visit
with God was not something she would out-
grow. As she relaxed, her left leg jerked, sending
Thunder Cave, the book she had been reading,
sliding to the floor. Her purple flashlight followed close behind, the beam of light shining
on the dark wall. Zoey, her long-haired, black-

and-white poodle and Pomeranian mix puppy, was already asleep with her nose tucked under Anna's covers. Tonight sleep came quietly.

Anna was jolted awake when she felt something cold crawling on her left foot. *Something's not right,* clicked into her brain, and her eyes jerked open. Two blue eyes and a smiling mouth were peering at her from the bottom of her bed, and Daniel's fingers were tickling her foot! Daniel giggled because he'd awakened his sister.

"Shh, Daniel, what are you doing?" she whispered. "If you value your life, you'd better not wake Zoey."

Daniel Mark was her nine-and-a-half-year-old brother. His blond hair was hanging in his face as his long, thin body crawled over the end of the bed. From deep in his throat came a growl as he shoved some of the stuffed animals over so he could sit on the bed. He was doing his animal thing again.

Now fully awake, Anna sat up and quickly checked her room to see if Daniel had messed with her things. She looked around, checking on Peter, her beloved gray rat, who was scratching in the shredded paper in the bottom of his cage. Her hermit crabs, Pinky and Methuselah, lay quietly in the cage by the window. The rest of the room was a zoo of stuffed animals ranging in size from the smallest, Zeke, her green Beanie Baby alligator, to Black Beauty, her thirty-six-inch-tall, black-and-white horse with a red, white, and blue scarf tied around its neck. Her great-great-grandmother's brown wooden desk sat in the corner covered with books and yesterday's jeans and red tee shirt. As her eyes moved around the room, she caught her reflection in the sliding mirrored doors on her closet. Her long, brownish blond hair, still wet from her nightly shower, hugged her face, and her blue eyes looked like black holes in the dim light from the hall. She thought she looked older than her twelve years.

A wide-awake Zoey joined the conversation when she started wagging her tail. Anna said with irritation in her voice, "Thanks a lot, Daniel. Now Zoey and I will never get back to sleep. This better be good. What do you want anyway?"

"Anna, I need to tell you something important, and it can't wait until tomorrow," replied Daniel.

"Sure," replied Anna, "that's what you always say. You just want to sleep in my room again. Why can't you sleep this time, bad dreams, weird sounds, or what?"

"Anna, you never, ever give me a chance. I do have something to tell you," insisted Daniel, "and it's about Grandma."

"Okay, tell me," she continued to whisper. "What about Grandma?"

"I had to go to the bathroom, and I decided to check on the parents on the way. As I was listening at their door, I heard the words *Anna, Daniel, Grandma,* and *Ryan.*

Then Mom said, "So, do we let them or not?"

"I was so scared they'd catch me listening I ran to the bathroom, and then I came straight here," continued Daniel. "What do you think is happening?"

"Let's go listen and see if we can hear more," Anna replied.

Both kids leapt off the bed, leaving Zoey alone. She ran to the edge of the bed, looked down, and started to whimper.

"Shh," said Anna again, this time to the dog. "I guess we'd better take her so she won't cry. I'll carry her because I'm the only one who can keep her quiet."

"No fair! I can do it! She's my dog too!" answered Daniel.

"Shh! Or we'll never hear what they're talking about," hissed his sister. "If you are quiet, I'll let you feed her tomorrow."

The two kids crept down the long, gold-carpeted hall until they came to their parents' bedroom door. In their house, all the bedroom doors were kept closed at night for fire safety. When their parents were younger, they had been volunteer firemen at work and knew the difference that closed doors could make during a fire. The kids knelt on the floor and put their ears against the door. They listened for the sound of their parents' voices or snoring. They had listened at this door many times hoping to hear what *the parents* were talking about. It was quiet in the bedroom, and Daniel whispered, "We're too late. They're asleep."

As they turned to walk back to Anna's room, they heard their dad say, "Well, I've thought about the trip, and it will be a family decision. Guess we should have a family meeting in the morning if we have time."

Quietly their mom said, "I know my mom will make the trip fun for them."

"And," their dad said, "it will be good for the cousins to spend some time together, Lynn."

Lynn replied, "I'm so exhausted. I've got to get some sleep. Can we talk about this tomorrow?"

"Sure, Lynn," came their father's reply. "Good night."

The kids waited until it was quiet again and then walked quickly back to Anna's room.

"I wonder what that's all about?" asked Anna.

"It obviously has something to do with Grandma and Ryan," added Daniel.

On the way back to her room Anna thought about their cousin Ryan from their mom's side of the family. He lived in Atlanta, Georgia. He was seven years old. He lived with his mom, Lea; his dad, Al; and baby brother, Brady. They didn't get to see them very often because they lived so far away. They mostly knew Ryan from phone calls centered on a special event, a vacation, birthdays, or other holidays, and sometimes they sent e-mails. Ryan seemed older than his seven-plus years because he was the same height as Daniel and Ryan acted older when he was around his cousins. Now Anna pictured him in her mind. His hair was as dark as Anna's and Daniel's was light; he had dark brown eyes, and he smiled and laughed a lot. Anna and Daniel enjoyed being with Ryan because he liked all of nature and was always ready for some fun.

Blond-haired, blue-eyed Brady, on the other hand, was into everything as he tried to keep up with the older kids. He kept everyone laughing with his winning smile and near catastrophes and determination to be a *big kid* too. Even though he was determined to be like the big kids, his body couldn't keep up. That made for an interesting time for Aunt Lea. Brady as a toddler was never boring.

Now, back in Anna's bedroom, brother and sister were sitting on Anna's bunk beds. Daniel had crawled up to the top bunk and had made a space for himself beside a stuffed lion and two tigers, a grey wolf, three black bears, several multicolored cats, three dogs, and two fish. His head was hanging over the edge as he watched Anna try to get Zoey settled one more time. However, it was not to be because Zoey started sniffing and walking in circles as she did when she was getting ready to pee. "Oh, geez," said Anna as she grabbed her dog. She ran out of her room, across the hall, and into the bathroom where Zoey's papers were.

Daniel climbed down from the top bunk and followed Anna. While they waited for the puppy to use her papers, Daniel got himself a drink from the faucet on the sink. He was an expert at drinking without using a glass. He kept his footstool with his name on it right by the sink so he could easily stick his mouth under the faucet. He was always thirsty and was proud of himself for saving paper cups. With water dripping down his face he said, "I think we should call Grandma tomorrow and ask her what's going on."

"Good idea, Daniel. Grandma will tell us if we ask her," encouraged his sister.

After Zoey was finished and Daniel was

watered, they returned to Anna's room. Anna looked at her brother and said, "Okay, you can sleep in here tonight. You did the right thing coming to tell me what you heard. We'll call Grandma first thing in the morning. Now remember, you can't mess around in here or you will die, so go to sleep." Daniel crawled back up on the top bunk, pushed the lion out of his way, and felt his eyes closing. Anna settled her baby dog again, and after telling herself five times to relax and to take deep breaths, she too fell asleep.

Grandma, the Riddler, Riddles

At seven the next morning, the sleeping kids were awakened by Zoey, who was licking Anna's face and making whimpering puppy sounds. Anna reached over and turned off her radio alarm clock. It had been set for 7:15 a.m., and she could have slept for fifteen more minutes. Sometimes she wondered why she bothered to set her alarm because something always happened to wake her up early. Lucky Daniel always slept longer than she did. Maybe Zoey would go back to sleep if she rubbed her belly. Anna kept her eyes tightly closed as she desperately tried to get the puppy to lie down and go back to sleep.

Meanwhile Daniel had started moving around on the top bunk, and Anna felt the bed move. He leaned over the edge of the bed. When he saw Zoey wiggling around, he laughed and said, "Anna, open your eyes. Zoey is going to pee on your hand. Remember, you're the only one who can take care of her."

Anna made a dash for the bathroom while her brother lay back in bed. A smile crossed his face as he thought how funny it would've been if Zoey had peed on his sister's hand. It would serve her right for not sharing their puppy more often.

Anna returned from the bathroom and said, "Daniel, I think we'd better talk about Grandma. Now we know this much. We know there is a trip and it has to do with Ryan, Grandma, and us. Next, we know it will be decided in our family meeting. Do you think we should still call Grandma?"

"Yes," replied Daniel, "and the sooner the better. What if Mom and Dad call the meeting during breakfast?"

"Okay then, this is what I think we should do," said Anna. "We will ask to call before we eat. We'll use the speakerphone in Mom's bedroom. You will need to be extra quiet so Mom and Dad won't hear what we say. I think you should be the one to go ask Mom for permission to call because she always says yes to you."

"Okay, but you always make me do the hard things because I'm the youngest," replied Daniel. "I think I heard Mom in the kitchen." And with that he ran down the stairs to his mother.

He came back with a smile on his face, "You were right. Mom said it was okay to call, but we have to be at the breakfast table in ten minutes."

Zoey tagged along as the kids headed to their parents' room to call. The number had been programmed into the phone, but each kid knew the number anyway. Their grandparents lived in Wyoming, and the area code was 307. They also knew Wyoming used mountain standard time, so it was always one hour later than the pacific standard time used in Long Beach, California, where they lived. Grandma had explained that time zones were like the sun; they started in the East and settled in the West. That helped the kids remember which way the time zones moved.

Grandma picked up the phone after the third ring. She was out of breath and answered by saying, "Hi, kids, is everything okay?"

"Grandma, how did you know it was us?" asked Daniel.

"I guessed," replied his grandma in a teasing voice.

"Grandma, I know you have caller ID on your phone. You can't fool us. Why are you out of breath?" asked Anna.

Grandma laughed and said, "I just came in the door from walking along Garden Creek Parkway with my friend Bridget. We saw two mountain lions, one bear, three eagles, six deer, and four rattlesnakes."

The kids rolled their eyes at each other, and Anna said, "Grandma, you're doing it to us again. You're teasing us. Be real."

Their grandma returned with, "Okay, we really, really saw three deer, one eagle flying overhead, and some insects buzzing around. I would've had more fun if I'd seen the rest of the animals, though. Now what are you kids doing this early in the morning? Don't you have school today?"

The grandkids both blurted out, "We heard Mom and Daddy talking last night."

"Okay," answered Grandma.

"And," Anna rushed on, "they said your name and ours."

"And Ryan's too," added Daniel.

"Anyway," Anna went on, "we want to know what's going on."

"Well, kids, I thought it would be fun to take a trip with you," answered Grandma.

Daniel asked, "Where are we going? Do Mom and Dad get to come too?"

"First things first, Daniel," she answered. "Are you guys up for an adventure? You will be going where your parents have never been! Our destination will be a surprise! You kids will solve riddles to find out where we are going. By the time we arrive at our destination, you will have learned many things about the city. Oops, I said city. See, I've already given you a clue. It's so hard for me to keep a secret.

"And no," she continued, "your parents are not coming. This trip will be for kids and Grandma because Grandpa has to work."

Anna asked, "When do we go, and do we get to miss school?"

"What do you think? You guys know I'd never take you out of school while it's in session unless it was an emergency. Think a minute, what holiday is coming up?" replied Grandma.

Daniel and Anna looked at each other, and Anna said, "In three weeks we have spring break. Is that when we're going?"

"But what about Ryan?" interrupted Daniel.

"It just so happens," added Grandma, "that Ryan's break is the same as yours."

"Wow!" exclaimed Daniel, "Did Mom and Dad say we could go?"

"I called your parents yesterday and asked them to think about the trip and then to discuss it with you," explained Grandma. "I did the same for Ryan and talked to your Aunt Lea. She and Uncle Al will decide if he can take the trip with us. It's too bad Brady isn't old enough to come, but we'll have other trips when he gets older."

"We expect Daddy to call a family meeting at breakfast this morning so they can talk about the trip," said Anna. "Now we have time to think of reasons to convince them we should go. It's almost time for us to go downstairs and eat breakfast. Bye, Grandma. We'll call you. I love you." With those words she pressed off, and the kids raced downstairs to eat.

The kids plopped down at the table in their favorite places. Anna always sat across from her mom, and Daniel sat on his dad's left. Their parents were already eating, so each kid quickly thanked God for the food and began eating Honey Bunches of Oats, their favorite cereal. They preferred the 2% milk their mother drank to the whole milk their dad drank, and Daniel would've added sugar if he could've gotten away with it. He thought you could never have enough sugar on cereal. However, Anna was more careful about what she put in her body.

She and her friends wanted to stay in shape for sports.

Dad finished swallowing his eggs, cleared his throat, and said, "It's about time you got here. You need to hurry so you won't be late for school."

Lynn joined in, "I wonder if we'll ever be able to eat without rushing. It seems we're always late. Mornings are so hard, and we must be on time. Do you think we have the time for a family meeting, David?"

The kids smiled because they had predicted this would happen. They quickly looked down at their bowls to hide their smiles. It was nice to know what Mom and Dad would do, but they didn't want their parents to know they were so predictable.

Their dad cleared his throat again and said, "Grandma called yesterday and invited you to take a trip with her over spring break. Would you be interested in going?"

The kids looked at each other and said in unison, "Yes!" Daniel added, "So where would Grandma take us?"

Their parents shook their heads at the question without answering and their dad stood up and reached for some more coffee. He looked tall to his children at his six feet two inches. His grey-green eyes looked back at them, and he smiled but didn't say a word. When their dad didn't answer, they looked to their short five foot three inch mom. Her brown eyes were sparkling because she knew something the kids didn't. She smiled as she answered Daniel's question about the destination by saying, "Grandma asked us not to tell you. We can only say that you would leave Thursday evening and would come back late Monday night. Your cousin Ryan is also invited to go, but Brady is too young."

"Wow!" Daniel said, "That would be great! I vote yes."

Anna, remembering the conversation from last night, added, "We haven't seen Ryan since Christmas, and we always have a good time with Grandma. We also learn a lot when we spend time with her and Grandpa. I vote yes too. What do you guys think?"

Looking up at Dad, Mom said, "We figured you'd want to go, but we wanted to check with you first. Daddy and I wish we were going, but we weren't invited. Grandma will call tonight for the answer, which I guess is a yes. Before we go, is everything okay with you kids? Do you have anything to add to our meeting?"

Both kids nodded their heads no to show that everything was okay. "If so," she continued, "Daniel, remember to wash your hands and face before you leave for school. I know you will wear your clean school uniform, but your body cleanliness is another matter."

Daniel, complaining, said, "Aw, Mom, you know how I hate to have water on my face except when I get a drink." After whining he gave her his most winning smile.

Dismissing him with a pat on his arm, his mom continued, "Remember to put Zoey in her kennel, Anna. By the way, did you feed Peter and the hermit crabs this morning?" With these words ringing in their ears, the kids raced upstairs to get ready for school.

How to Rule your School

The first bell was ringing when Anna and Daniel entered the school building. They were two of the same group of students who often hurried in at the last minute. Each kid knew there were five minutes left until the tardy bell rang. Daniel hustled off toward his classroom with his friend Regan close behind. Regan had been waiting for Daniel at the door as he did every morning. He greeted Daniel with, "It's about time."

And Daniel answered with, "You know how slow my mom is." The boys made it to their desks before the tardy bell rang.

Anna, on the other hand, looked in the office door as she went by and noticed the secretary, Mrs. Barnett, coming out with a new girl. The girl seemed to be about Anna's age, but she was taller. Anna smiled and turned to Mrs. Barnett and said, "Hi, Mrs. Barnett."

Mrs. Barnett answered back, "Hi, Anna, this is Mandi, our new student. She's going to be in Mrs. Andrew's room with you. Would you show Mandi around?"

Anna smiled again and said, "Hi and welcome to our school. It's hard to be the new kid, but I think you will like it here. Most of the teachers are fun, and we get to do great projects. Some of the kids are really nice, and others, well, you will find out for yourself. I'll be glad to show you to our room." Mrs. Barnett said good-bye and left the two girls at the door of their sixth grade classroom.

Mandi followed Anna into the room and

then walked up to the teacher's desk. All of her new classmates stopped working, and it got very quiet. They all turned to look at her. The new girl was fair game.

Mrs. Andrew introduced Mandi to the kids and had her sit in the empty desk next to Anna. Mandi looked at the other twenty-five students and noticed they were working on an assignment written on the white board in the front of the room. Mrs. Andrew looked at the class and said, "Nice job, class. You started working on your Daily Oral Language as soon as you came into the room. Mandi, each morning we begin by practicing our language skills. In our class everyone is expected to do all of the work all of the time. In order to do this, every student must spend the time necessary to complete the activity. We value this time and call it 'time on task.' When I say 'time on task,' everyone knows to stay busy. If you finish your work early, the time is yours and you can choose how you spend it. There's only one rule: you must not interfere with other students and their work. There can be no arguments or you lose this privilege. Today the assignment consists of incorrectly written sentences. You need to write them correctly. You will also see some reading vocabulary words listed on the board. Please read the words. If there are any you don't know, look them up in the student dictionary in your desk. You will be tested on these words later. When you are finished, check your answers with the answer guide located in the front of the room. Please correct your mistakes. Do you understand, Mandi?"

Mandi said "yes," and following the lead of the other students, she began working. She, like Anna, finished early. After finishing she was able to get a good look around the room. A banner that said "Sixth grade Rules: Be a Role Model" was hung over the white board. At her old school, most of the sixth graders were anything but role models. They thought rules didn't apply to them because they were the oldest students in the school. Sometimes they acted worse than younger students in the lower grade levels. Mandi wondered what being a role model meant to the kids at this school. She knew she'd find out sooner or later. She also noticed a bulletin board that said "It's Smart to be Bilingual," and it had Spanish vocabulary words all over it with pictures to match. Mandi was pleased to know she would continue learning a second language here.

Anna interrupted Mandi's thoughts about Spanish when she introduced her to Allison and Katie. Mrs. Andrew allowed friends to sit near one another until a problem arose. Today the girls whispered quietly while they waited for the rest of the class to finish the Daily Oral Language assignment. They learned Mandi had a younger sister named Mikayla. They also learned Mandi liked to play volleyball and was on the A team at her old school. They would welcome her to their team because she was so tall.

Anna's favorite things at school were her friends, math, Spanish, and lunch. This was her day for Spanish class with Señora Giraldo. This was her fourth year of learning the language, and she was getting better at speaking it. Sometimes she and Allison and David practiced their Spanish at lunch. It gave them a good feeling to know and understand a language other kids didn't understand. Knowledge was power, after all.

Today lunch time seemed to arrive quickly. Anna joined Allison and David at their table. Anna said, "*¿Ves a esas muchachas allá? Se llaman Lacy y Sarah. Lacy lleva el suéter rojo. Nos esta mirando. A ella le gusta Kyle.*" ("See the girls over there? Their names are Lacy and Sarah. Lacy is the one in the red sweater. She is watching us. She likes Kyle.") Allison and David smiled because they liked being voyeurs.

Later Mrs. Kingston, the lunchroom aide, walked over and stood next to them. Allie said, "*Cuidado; la señora Kingston parece estar enojada hoy.*" ("Watch out; Mrs. Kingston looks grouchy today.")

Then David said, "*Siempre está enojada.*" ("She is grouchy most days.")

Still practicing, Anna added, "*Mira a Kendra, Robyn, y Jennifer discutiendo. No sé cómo pueden ser mejor amigas. Debe ser difícil con tres.*" ("Look at Kendra, Robyn, and Jennifer arguing. They sure have a hard time being best friends. Guess it's harder with three.") The three girls had no idea Anna was talking about them.

As much as the rest of Anna's school day was the same, Daniel's was a different story. Every day for Daniel was an adventure. He especially liked science, music, and social studies. He couldn't seem to keep his desk organized and often kept things like his secret codebook for writing notes and his collection of dried earthworms inside his desk. He kept the earthworms because he knew it freaked out some of the kids.

He kept his water bottle under his desk. This water bottle was always filled because he never knew when his brain would get thirsty. His teacher, Mrs. Lange, had told the class that brain research showed test scores went up when the brain was hydrated. Daniel had known about hydration since he was four years old. He'd learned about it by watching a Rescue Heroes video. Now Mrs. Lange and some of the parents furnished the water bottles once a week. He believed if a little water would do the trick, a whole lot more might do better. Besides, sometimes he just couldn't sit still any longer, and a trip to the drinking fountain to fill his water bottle was just what he needed to get himself back on track.

He had decided to do a science experiment

to see which kids drank water and if those kids got good grades. His scientific question was: Will drinking water at school help you get good grades? For three days he'd kept a class list in his desk, and if he saw a classmate take a drink, he'd put a tally mark by his or her name. Everyone knew which kids usually got the best scores, and then Daniel compared the tally marks of the *smart* kids to the other kids. So far he hadn't come to any conclusions, but he drank the water anyway. He never said anything to the other kids, but he knew he was one of those *smart* kids because he also earned good grades.

Today had been uneventful until music class. He liked his music teacher because she was nice to her students and she told funny jokes. Best of all, Mrs. Jones seemed to like Daniel back. In the fourth grade musical, Daniel had the part of Danny Boy because he was a good singer and would learn his lines. His friends, Jamie and Regan, thought he got the part because his name was Daniel, but Mrs. Jones and Daniel knew the real reason.

Practice for the upcoming class play went

so well that Mrs. Jones gave all the kids a piece of hard candy. Daniel chose a round red and white piece as he walked out the door of the music room. He forgot he had the candy until he was sitting in his classroom desk. When he remembered it, he put it into his mouth. He usually chewed his candy as fast as his teeth could break it up, but this time he decided to take his time eating it. He had tasted the mint flavor for about three minutes when he decided to take a drink of water to see if the taste would get stronger. It tasted better, and he took a big suck. That was when the candy got stuck in his throat.

Things happened very quickly after that. He tried harder and harder to swallow, and when he couldn't, he got out of his desk and walked to the drinking fountain in the back of the room. He heard Regan say, "Mrs. Lange, something's wrong with Daniel."

Immediately after hearing those words, Daniel felt Mrs. Lange beside him. He felt tingly and couldn't take a breath even though he kept trying. He bent over the sink and was grasping for the drinking fountain when Mrs. Lange said, "Daniel, I'm going to do the Heimlich on you. It might hurt a little." She stood behind him, and making a two-handed fist, she placed it just below his sternum. She pulled him hard against her.

His brain had begun to click out when he felt another quick shove against his chest. Another much harder shove came next and Daniel felt the candy fly out of his mouth, and he heard the candy land in the sink! He took a deep breath and then another. It felt so good to be able to breathe again!

Mrs. Lange sat him in a chair while she called the nurse on the classroom phone. It seemed like just seconds when Mrs. DeCastro, the school nurse, and Principal Park hurried into the classroom. Mrs. Park asked, "Daniel, are you all right?" Daniel nodded his head yes. He didn't say so, but he did feel a little shaky and weak as the nurse checked him over. His body seemed to be okay, but the adults walked with him to the nurse's office to check him further and to call his parents. Mrs. DeCastro listened to his lungs and checked his throat to see if it was scratched. She gave him a drink to see if he swallowed okay and then called his mom's cell-phone number. His mom didn't answer, so they called his dad at work.

After hearing Mrs. Park's story, his dad asked to talk to Daniel. Daniel explained that Mrs. Lange had saved his life and he was going to be just fine. He hung up, told Mrs. Park one more time that he was okay, and then he started back to his classroom. On his way back to class, he breathed a quick prayer thanking God for taking care of him.

The rest of the class gave him a standing ovation as he came into the classroom, and Daniel gave them a deep bow. Then he and Mrs. Lange and the class had a discussion about what had happened. Mrs. Lange wanted the class to learn several things from the accident. Number one was how quickly accidents can happen, even when you are doing the right thing. Number two was how important it was not to panic but to remain calm, to keep your cool, during a scary time. Number three was how important it was for Regan to call for his teacher's help when he had noticed Daniel was having trouble breathing. And number four was a reminder that when the going gets tough, the tough get going. The class laughed at the fourth one because they had heard it many times from Mrs. Lange. They usually joined in to finish the verse by saying, "the tough get going."

When he returned to his desk, he found the piece of candy wrapped in a paper towel. He looked at Mrs. Lange and mouthed, "Thank you." However, he did not finish eating the red and white mint candy. He put it next to his codebook and his worms in his desk, where it would be safe.

After all the excitement, the class continued working in their guided reading groups until 3:20 p.m., when the bell rang to dismiss school. Mrs. Lange reminded her class of the homework assignment. After writing it down in their daily planning books, Daniel and Regan walked out of the class door, grabbed their backpacks, and headed for the exit doors. Regan's ride was already there, so he ran to the car, and Daniel looked around for his ride.

The Relationships
of the Relations

Daniel spotted Anna, and they hurried to Katie's blue Chrysler van. Katie's mom was the carpool driver for the week, and Katie was already waiting in the car. On the way home, Katie and Anna talked about Mandi and how hard it would be to be the new kid in school, especially this late in the school year. After a ten-minute ride, they reached Anna and Daniel's house, and the two kids leapt out of the van. They said a quick thank you and ran to the front door of their house. Anna removed the key from inside the front pocket in her backpack and unlocked the door.

While Anna went to get Zoey out of her large kennel in the garage, Daniel ran to the kitchen to see what his mom had left for a snack. He was starving and thirsty, so it would be an emergency until he fed his stomach. Situated on the counter next to the microwave was a bag of microwave popcorn and a note. The kids were to drink the apple juice in the refrigerator and eat the popcorn. Mom would be home from her part-time job at four fifteen. Daniel put the bag in the microwave, punched in two minutes and thirty seconds, and waited. Since he wasn't too good at waiting, he checked the black and white, cat-shaped cookie jar. He decided that one chocolate-chip cookie wouldn't hurt, and he ate it in three bites.

Anna came into the kitchen with Zoey in her arms. She kissed her puppy several times and then put her on the floor. Zoey made her rounds sniffing in all the corners. If she found some food on the floor, she would be happy.

By the time Daniel had the juice out and had taken a drink, the popcorn was done. Both kids made a dash for the microwave. The first kid to open the bag got the first bite. This bite tasted the best because it tasted and smelled like butter. However, there was one hazard. The person opening the sack could also be burned from the escaping steam inside the bag. It was a matter of who should be first, younger brother or older sister, so the risk of a little pain was worth it. As usual Anna won because she was bigger and she blocked Daniel from the microwave.

"That's not fair. I'm telling Mom," complained Daniel.

"You go right ahead, and I'll tell her you ate cookies," replied Anna.

"I did not," countered Daniel.

"Yes you did. I heard you put the lid on the cookie jar. I'll bet if I checked your mouth there would be chocolate in it."

"There's no chocolate in my mouth," denied Daniel.

"Then you swallowed it because I heard the cookie jar lid," insisted his sister.

After each kid had eaten several bites of popcorn, Anna walked over to the answering machine to check the messages. The red light was blinking, so she knew someone had called. With pencil and notepad in hand, she pressed the message button.

Message number one was someone from the church wanting to speak to her dad. Anna wrote the number down and listened to message number two. It was from Ryan in Atlanta. He said, "Hey, Anna and Daniel, why aren't you home? I need to talk to you. Bye."

Message number three was Ryan again. He said, "Too bad for you guys. I guess you realize I've been home from school for three hours. Aren't I lucky? Where are you?"

Message number four was, "I know our time is three hours ahead of yours, but this is taking too long. Call me as soon as you get home. By the way, did you know vampire bats don't suck blood? They lap it up. Really! Call me."

The kids looked at each other and laughed. Ryan was always looking for something interesting about animals. He had two aquariums of tropical fish in his house. One tank had brackish water and the other tank had fresh water in it. His favorite kind of fish was an African cichlid called a convict because it was striped and it ate other fish. Ryan said they were ferocious. He knew lots of unusual facts about fish, such as flying fish don't really fly but are gliding and fish don't drink water even though they open and close their mouths while swimming.

Anna turned on the TV to the Discovery Channel to wait for her mom to come home. At ten minutes after four, the kids heard the garage door opening and knew their mom had arrived. Now they could call Ryan.

Their mom was flushed as she came rushing through the door carrying her usual two bags of groceries. Their dad bought most of the groceries on Saturday morning, but for one reason or another they had to go back during the week. She went in and kissed each kid on the top of the head as they were watching bears eating salmon somewhere in Alaska. She turned the TV off to a chorus of, "Mom, we're watching that!"

Mom said, "I turned it off because I want to know about school today. Daniel, are you okay? Daddy called me. What happened?"

"What do you mean what happened?" asked Anna.

By now all three were in the kitchen, and Anna and Daniel were helping Mom put the groceries away. Daniel answered his mother with, "Mrs. Lange saved my life today. Here's proof." With that said, Daniel pulled the piece of candy wrapped in the paper towel out of his pocket and showed it to his mom. The candy made the story real, and Lynn grabbed Daniel and gave him a big hug.

Anna looked at the candy and said, "What's going on? I want to know too."

Their mom continued to hug Daniel and said, "Tell us the whole story and don't leave out any of the details." They stopped working and sat down at the kitchen table while Daniel told his story. Anna interrupted him several times by saying, "Geez!" but Lynn didn't say anything until Daniel ended with, "And then I talked to Dad."

Lynn looked up and said, "Thank you, God, for guardian angels. Now let me see your throat." With those words she proceeded to look into his mouth and to feel the outside of his throat. She ended the search by saying, "I wonder if we should take you to the doctor to make sure everything's all right."

After another hug from his mother, Daniel said, "Mom, I'm just fine. What can I eat? I'm starving."

Mom replied, "If you can eat popcorn, I guess your throat is okay, but popcorn is all you can have until dinner. I don't want you to ruin your appetite. Daddy's going to be late getting home because he has a meeting after work."

Daniel moaned, "Please, please I'm starving! I will eat my dinner, I promise." And with those words he added his saddest look and then reached over and gave his mom his special hug that made her feel like her guts would fall out. His mother could never say no to his saddest face and that hug.

She shrugged and said, "Okay, I guess you can have an orange. Here I'll cut it in half for you."

Anna asked, "Could I have one too?" Lynn handed another orange to Anna as Anna added, "Were you scared when you choked, Daniel? I would've been. Geez, I'm glad you're okay."

Daniel answered, "Anna, you know I'm never scared." And then he laughed.

Anna continued, "Mom, Ryan called. Can we call him back?"

Her mom had already started fixing dinner. Anna hoped they were having some kind of pasta with cheese. She'd eat anything with mozzarella or cheddar cheese in it. On the other hand, Daniel always checked the color of the cheese. If it was white or light orange cheese he would eat it but he refused to eat dark orange cheese because it tasted *awful,* and sometimes to be dramatic he said the word *gross.*

Lynn replied, "Sure, go ahead." And both kids raced out of the room to their parents' bedroom.

The phone had only rung two times when Ryan answered the phone. Both cousins said, "Hi, Ryan."

Ryan interrupted with, "Can you go?"

Anna and Daniel both yelled, "Yes! Can you?"

"Yes," said Ryan, "I can, but I really had to work hard to convince my parents. I begged and whined. I didn't have to cry but almost. It helped that Grandma would already be here. My mom has to consult on a trial that week so she will be really stressed and busy, and my dad asked a million questions about the trip. You know how he wants to know all the details and how concerned he is about safety. He checks and double-checks everything. When he asked questions, I said, 'I don't know yet, but I'll ask Grandma.' That's the only answer I could give him because Grandma hasn't told us her plan. I just got off the phone with Grandma, and she said an adventure is waiting for us! She's going to call you guys tonight. We have to figure out where we're going on our trip by solving riddles, but I can't tell you any more because she wants to tell you."

"Did she give you any hints?" asked Anna. "Maybe it's Disney World."

"I hope we get to go on rides," added Daniel.

"Grandma just said she would e-mail us riddles to help us figure out where we're going. I can't talk because it's time for me to go to bed. Do you guys know that fish sleep with their eyes wide open? Bye." And before either of his cousins could answer, Ryan hung up.

The kids in California knew it was time to do homework before dinner, so they went back to the kitchen. Each kid had a desk in his or her bedroom, but they usually did homework at the kitchen table so Mom or Dad could help. Besides, the saying *misery loves company* seemed to apply to doing homework. Tonight Daniel had twenty math problems to do using pre-algebra, and Anna had to write a five-paragraph personal narrative about what she would like to do during spring break. They did lots of writing in sixth grade.

They'd just gotten started when the phone rang. Lynn answered, and after talking a few minutes, she said, "Kids, Grandma wants to talk to you."

Daniel said, "We'll go upstairs to your bedroom to talk on the speakerphone. I sure wish we had a speakerphone down here." With that said, both kids ran upstairs.

On the way up, Anna thought about her grandma. She knew lots of things about her. She and Grandpa had retired from their jobs. Grandma had been a second and third grade teacher. She had loved her students and her job. She said she had been changing the world one student at a time. As for Grandpa, he had worked at a college for a long time, and he got a building named after him. Anna knew how old Grandma was, she knew her favorite thing was to travel, she knew she liked to walk and hike most anywhere and to ride bicycles on bike trails. However, what Anna liked most was that her grandma loved her no matter what happened. That went for her grandpa too. When Anna got worried about something, which was often, or got into trouble, which happened sometimes, she knew Grandma would understand. Grandma didn't tell her what to do but would listen to her. Then she would ask some questions about Anna's problem. Answering the questions seemed to help Anna make a decision. Sometimes Anna made the right decisions, and sometimes she made mistakes. Her grandma often said, "Anna, everyone makes mistakes. Smart people learn from those mistakes." That was another thing. Her grandma quoted sayings like, "What you do speaks so loudly, I can't hear what you say," and "Beauty is in the eyes of the beholder." When she said that, she always ended with "And, Anna, you know you are always beautiful to me."

The kids had reached the bedroom, and Daniel picked up the phone and punched the speaker. Daniel said, "Hi, Grandma. Guess what! Did you know we get to go on a trip with you!"

Grandma said. "Hi to you both, and yeah! I talked to Ryan, and do I have a deal for you! Do you remember the saying 'Where there's a will, there's a way?' Well my question is, do you have the will for an adventure? Tonight I also want you to think about this saying 'The journey makes the destination better.' I've e-mailed you guys and Ryan with the first step in our journey. Each day you will get further directions and hints on your e-mail. Since both of you have e-mail addresses, I will alternate between you when I write. Whichever one I send the day's message to should answer. I know you don't like typing with the correct fingering, but I want you to use your keyboarding skills. It will be good practice for you both. We only have three weeks until spring break. We have a lot to do. Today I sent the message to you,

Anna. Tomorrow I will send it to you, Daniel. Grandpa is waiting for me, so I need to go. I love you both. Good-bye. Remember, the journey makes the destination better."

Both children said, "Love you and good-bye." And Daniel hung up the phone.

"What do you think Grandma means by 'the journey makes the destination better,' and 'we must have the will to find the way?" asked Daniel as the kids started back down the stairs to finish their homework.

"Well we know that *destination* means where we are going and the *journey* is how we get there. As for the *will* part, I think Grandma is trying to teach us something again. We'll have to wait and see what it is," replied his sister.

The Journey and the Destination

When the kids came back into the kitchen, dinner was ready, and their dad was setting the table. They greeted him and gave him a quick hug. The kids were always happy and excited to see him. When he was home, he was usually busy working on a project, and many times he let his children help him. If he wasn't working in his garden or in the kitchen, they would usually find him in his shop in the garage. He was a good builder and had just made each of them a little, oak-stained wooden box with a pull-out drawer. His gift was a place to keep treasures, and the kids would keep this treasure chest forever. The treasures might change, but the boxes would always be there, just like their dad.

Anna and Daniel raced through dinner. They rushed because they knew they had to finish their homework before they could use the computer to check Grandma's message. Homework would be easier now that Grandma had given Anna something to write about. The title of her narrative would be "The Mysterious Trip."

After being dismissed from the kitchen table, Anna and Daniel carried their dirty dishes to the sink, rinsed them, and put them in the dishwasher. Then the kids took their homework to the dining-room table to finish their assignments.

They continued working until the phone rang. Meghan and Allie called Anna, but the rule was homework had to be finished before time could be spent on the phone. Daniel finished early. The math problems were easy. When his friend Trey called to check answers on the problems with Daniel, Daniel had missed one, and Trey had missed two problems. Mrs. Lange encouraged her students to check answers with each other or with parents after completing homework. She wanted them to know two things about the homework. She wanted each student to know which problems were missed so they could understand why the mistakes were made and then to learn from those mistakes. She hoped they would not make the same mistakes on a test. It took a few minutes for Daniel to explain why his answers were correct and for Trey to convince Daniel that Daniel had missed one.

Anna, on the other hand, was struggling to finish her story. She didn't mind writing the story, but she hated to check her work for spelling and punctuation errors. Paragraphing was not easy either. The character part was easy. This story was about three cousins taking a trip with their grandma. She didn't know where they were going, but she decided she'd make them go somewhere she'd like to go. She'd like to go to a ranch so she could ride horses. She was a pretty good rider because she'd ridden horses at her Uncle Paul's church camp since she was a little kid.

Daniel reminded Anna to stay focused. He was finished; Anna wasn't finished. Maybe she needed his help. He could whip out a five-paragraph narrative easily. Brother and sister managed to compete in most everything. Daniel had been determined to be the first finished. He said, "It's easy to see who the smartest kid in this family is. Boys rule."

Anna pushed Daniel and said, "Boys rule only if their sisters let them!" They both laughed, and Anna finished quickly and asked their mom to look at the homework so the kids could put it into their backpacks. After checking for neatness and correct answers, Mom gave her permission to use the computer.

Dad was using the computer when the kids went into the family office to check Anna's e-mail. It seemed this always happened. One of the parents was already using the computer whenever the kids wanted to use it. They'd had a family meeting about this problem, and after much discussion it was still a problem. Anna and Daniel wanted a computer for themselves. Their parents couldn't afford another one because Mom only worked part time. Other kids had their own computers, but Lynn and David felt things like family vacations were more important. The family had to pick and choose where to spend their money. Tonight Dad decided he could finish after Anna and Daniel had gone to bed. He saved his work and let the kids have the computer.

Since they were accessing Anna's e-mail account, Anna got to use the computer while Daniel watched. There had been several arguments about who got to use the computer when, but the kids didn't want to risk getting their computer privileges taken away, so they hadn't told their parents.

Anna accessed her mail and made Daniel turn his head so he wouldn't see her password. It was her secret, and she was the only one who knew it. It was written on a piece of paper and kept in a folder. Her parents kept that folder in the locked file cabinet in the office where they kept other important information.

It had been during one of their family meetings that the "Rules for Computer Use" were
set up. The kids knew these rules were set up to
protect them and to keep them safe. Number
one was: never open an e-mail message from
an address that you don't recognize. This pro-
tected against viruses and pornographic material. Anna and Daniel knew what pornography
was and how it could harm them. This rule also
saved time with spam and the hated cookies.
The kids knew their parents trusted them to
follow this rule and that if this trust was broken
computer privileges would be taken away until
the trust was earned back. If someone couldn't
be trusted with little things, no one would trust
them with big things. Other rules pertained to
chat rooms and doing research on the Web.
The search engines were bookmarked so they
could click on the search engine they desired.

Anna clicked on the message from her
grandma, and it said:

Hi kids—our adventure begins when we
fly to the largest state in the contiguous
states. What does contiguous mean? I

will be at Ryan's house, so he and I will fly together. The two of you will leave LAX Airport and fly directly to our destination. Ryan and I will meet you at your gate when you get off the plane. You will have a cell phone in case something unexpected happens. I will have my cell phone so we can talk to each other. Remember you are not allowed to use your phone until the flight attendant tells you it's okay. When we land we will be 140 miles from the Gulf of Mexico. There is a good chance that it will rain while we are there because thunderstorms and rain occur during every month. It rains the most in May and Sept. This city gets twenty-nine inches of rain every year. Can you believe it? That's about 2 ½ rulers stacked end to end. Where are we going, and do you have the will? Love to you both.

The kids looked at each other, and Anna said, "Daniel, do you understand Grandma's message?"

Daniel said with fear and excitement in his voice, "Anna, you and I are going to fly by ourselves for the first time. Now that's an adventure! Do you think Mom and Dad will let us?"

Anna replied, "Daniel. I'm twelve years old. On my next birthday I will be a teenager. I am old enough to fly by myself. Besides, we'll be together, and we're flying straight there. We'll be fine."

"Okay, but, Anna, what will I do all that time on the airplane?" asked her little brother.

"You can take your video games, and there are always books to read. Maybe they'll even have a movie, and we can take snacks. We'll get sodas and pretzels and cookies on the plane. Remember how it was when we flew with Dad and Mom? Daniel, this will be so fun. Where do you think we're going? I know the state already. Do you?"

"Of course I know, Anna. It's Texas. We had to do a state report in social studies, and Carly did Texas. That's the largest state that borders other states in the United States. Contiguous states mean states that touch each other. You didn't think I knew that, did you? I know a lot you don't think I know."

"Okay, okay," continued Anna, "I can't remember many cities in Texas, but I know about Houston because that's where Great-aunt Sam lives. Could that be where we're going?"

The kids read the e-mail again. "Grandma says it's 140 miles from the Gulf of Mexico. Let's look at a map," said Anna.

Daniel reached for the book of maps. It was on the shelf next to the computer table where all reference material was kept. Their dad insisted the *Webster's Dictionary,* a world atlas, a book of frequently misspelled words, and a book of synonyms be kept together. The kids could also use tools in their word-processing software but preferred a book because they could keep their place easier. Anna sometimes read the dictionary for fun because she loved learning new words. Daniel thought she was crazy. He didn't know any other sister who read the dictionary for fun. When they used one of the books, the kids always had to put it back in the same spot, or they would be in trouble with their parents. This was one of the times they were glad it was easy to find the book they wanted.

Daniel opened the *Rand McNally Easy to Read Travel Atlas*. The maps were in alphabetical order, and he found Texas on pages forty-six and forty-seven. It was easy to find the Gulf of Mexico, but Anna had to help him find the mileage legend in the right-hand corner. Together they started looking for cities that would be 140 miles away. They ruled out Corpus Christie because it was right on the coast. Brownsville, Galveston, and Texas City were ruled out for the same reason. Houston was only about forty miles away, and the same went with Beaumont.

"It just has to be San Antonio," said Anna.

"What about Austin?" asked Daniel. "Can we wait until tomorrow to decide? I'm tired."

As Daniel left the room, Zoey padded in with her tail wagging her body. She was irresistible. Anna picked her up and spent the next few minutes getting sloppy puppy kisses. Zoey was always happy to see her. Oh, how she loved this dog.

She clicked on reply to begin her message to Grandma. She started typing. She wrote:

Dear Grandma, Zoey says hi! Daniel was too tired to write to you tonight, so it will just be me. We think we're going to Texas. We're not sure which city we're going to. We think maybe it is San Antonio??? We know it's not Houston because that's not 140 miles from the Gulf of Mexico. Love, Anna

Quickly she pressed send, checked to see if the message had been sent, and then she shut down the computer. She grabbed Zoey, and the two of them went upstairs to get ready for bed. She was wired just thinking about the trip. She was anxious about flying alone with her brother, but Daniel could never know, or he might chicken out on the trip. They were going to have fun, and it had been interesting to look at the map with Daniel. Her younger brother might be smart after all. He'd known right where Texas and the Gulf of Mexico were.

After saying her good nights and taking Zoey to the bathroom, Anna decided to read. Reading often worked to help her wind down and then to help her get to sleep. *Thunder Cave* was a good book. Jacob Lanza was really brave to go to Kenya looking for his dad. If he could do that, she could ride on an airplane alone with her brother. Right now Jacob was riding his zebra-painted bicycle into what sounded like a desert. He'd already been robbed and beaten, and she wondered what would happen next. She settled Zoey, checked the other animals, crawled into bed, turned on her reading light, and started to read about Kenya.

Cousin Ryan and Sibling Brady

The next morning Ryan awoke to music coming from his alarm clock. It was 7:30 a. m., and the music sounded like water running and birds chirping. He would've preferred other music, but this was the music on his digital clock, and it was the same every morning. Listening to the music made him think how nice it would be to sleep in. He thought if he could sleep just a little longer he would be happier about this new day. However, he knew from experience that his little brother and his mom would be coming to check on him. If he was not up, his mom had been known to leap on his bed or to tickle his feet, or worse yet, to blow in his face until he opened his eyes. Mostly she gave him kisses all over his head until he woke up. Brady loved to join her in the game. Brady woke up early, and at three years old he never let his mom out of his sight. Where his mom was there was his little brother.

In extreme cases of his "Do I really have to get up?" disease, Ryan's dad would come into the bedroom and say, "Ryan, why aren't you up?" Then Ryan would get up because he never wanted to disappoint his dad. He didn't like to disappoint his mom either, but his mother was a softy when it came to him.

The sun was shining in his face as he looked across his bedroom to check on his fish in the aquarium. It made him happy just to look at this special place. His whole room was decorated as if it were in the ocean. The walls looked like schools of bright yellow fish; some big grouper fish, a whale, and two sharks were swimming around. His favorite fish, the convict, was swimming with some sunfish, and they had no idea how much danger they were in. Ryan smiled to himself. He was just crawling out of his double bed when his mom came through the door. He'd known it! He snuggled back into his covers and waited for her attack. He could tell she was ready for work because her dark brown hair was combed and she was wearing work clothes. "Watch out for these lips. Here they come," she said with a laugh. And with that she grabbed him and proceeded to give him what seemed like a million kisses. He wiggled and squirmed and giggled. He liked starting the day this way, and his mom knew it. Ryan knew one thing for sure: his best friends, Tommy and Aaron, could never know how he started the day because they would never stop teasing him.

"I'm awake. I'm awake," he said as he rolled over to the side of the bed and stood up on the floor. His mom knew that once he hit the floor he was good to go. He hugged her and said, "What's for breakfast? I'm hungry."

"Pancakes and worms are cooking on the stove. Hustle," she replied.

He smiled and said, "I prefer my pancakes without the worms, thank you." His mom smiled, gave him a pat on the head, and left the room. Ryan shuffled into the bathroom, pulling on his clothes as he walked. He'd laid out his clothes last night so he could hustle into them this morning. He didn't want to waste time deciding what to wear so he could spend more time eating breakfast. He was always hungry, so breakfast was the most important way to start the day. He had weighed over nine pounds when he was born and was a pretty good eater. It was a good thing his parents were good cooks. Dad mostly cooked on the weekends, and he and Ryan enjoyed watching cooking shows on TV. Both parents encouraged him to eat healthy. His mom usually cooked breakfast. He hoped it really was a pancake day.

He finished pulling his shirt over his head and walked into the kitchen eating area. His mom looked him over from head to toe. She was checking to make sure he didn't look as if "no one loved him." He knew this meant his clothes had to be clean and he couldn't wear his favorite shirt two days in a row unless it had been washed. The shirt was an athletic shirt that had a football helmet and the word *Patriots* on it. He was a fan of the *Patriots* because his dad had grown up in Boston.

At night his mom would sniff at him and say, "Ryan, you smell sweaty. Do you need a shower?" She knew he only showered when she made him and then he finished his shower quickly. He was too busy to take the time to do a good job at scrubbing. Besides, by the time it was 8:30 p.m. Ryan was so tired he just wanted to go to sleep.

He'd thought about doing what his friend Lane had done. Lane had sneaked his dad's cologne and tried to cover up his sweaty smell. He had come to school smelling like Stetson for Men! Their friend Kayston had liked it, but Ryan had laughed and scrunched up his nose. He said, "Way to go, Lane. Now you have two smells: Stetson for Men and sweat!" Lane had laughed, and now that was a private joke between them. When things got boring, Lane would sniff and ask, "Are you a man?" and the boys would crack up.

As Ryan was sitting down at the kitchen table, his dad walked into the room carrying Brady. At birth Brady weighed almost nine pounds, and he had grown like crazy. Everyone thought he was older than he was because of his size. He was really too big to carry, but his parents still carried him anyway because it was faster than waiting for Brady to walk. His dad said good morning to Ryan, and Brady crawled down from his dad's arms and ran over to sit next to Ryan at the table. Brady looked at his mom and said, "I want to eat pancakes too."

Like most little brothers, Brady was happiest when he could dress like, eat like, and act like his older brother. Brady was born looking a lot like Ryan. He had the same chin but had blue eyes and straight blond hair. Brady loved it when Ryan was playing with him and he was the center of everyone's attention. He didn't much like sharing Ryan with Ryan's friends, and their fights came when Brady wouldn't leave Ryan alone. Ryan loved his little brother, but he could remember when he had been the center of attention from his parents. When he had complained to his mom that it seemed like

Brady got all the attention, she'd told him there were pluses and minuses to everything, especially with little brothers. She said, yes, little brothers were a pain sometimes, but at least there would always be someone to play with. Ryan had to agree, but sometimes he wished Brady was older. Brady missed out on a lot of things because of his age. However, as the baby of the family, he did get the most attention. His mom was always saying, "Ryan, watch out for Brady. He's not as big as you are." And when Brady cried, everyone in the whole house came running to see what was wrong.

Ryan looked over at his dad, who was now standing in the doorway ready to go to work. He had court today, so he was ready early. Ryan knew his dad and mom worked very hard and that his dad helped people who had problems with the law. Some days it was really late when he came home from work, and they didn't get to eat dinner together; but his dad always made sure he was there whenever Ryan had a game or some other school activity. He and Ryan also roughhoused a lot. In their family that meant the brothers and dad wrestled and tried to pin each other to the floor. They would roll over and over. His mom often joined in, and the whole thing was great fun. When Ryan was little, this special time usually ended with blowing on someone's stomach. Usually it was either Dad or Mom's stomach because Ryan did the blowing. Now it was Brady blowing and Ryan watching because Ryan thought he was too old to do such baby stuff.

The roughhousing usually ended up with all of them shooting baskets in their driveway. Brady even had his own little hoop, but he always wanted to play with the rest of the family. The parents took turns holding Brady up so he could shoot baskets. His mom said shooting baskets was a way to let off steam and wind down. That made Ryan laugh. He could just see steam coming out of his parents' eyes, ears, noses, and mouths. They didn't know why he laughed when she said that, and he didn't tell them. They just had to wonder why he always laughed at that statement.

As Ryan and Brady ate their pancakes, their mom reminded them to eat some bacon and some scrambled eggs. She insisted they have some protein in the morning so they wouldn't get so hungry before lunch. Ryan hardy ever turned down more food and gladly ate two pieces of bacon and a few bites of the eggs. He knew he had thirty minutes to eat and to get to school. He also knew he had to hurry before Aaron got to his house. He, Tommy, and Aaron walked to school together.

"Earth to Ryan, Earth to Ryan, finish eating your breakfast," came his mother's voice. With those words Ryan started to pay attention to his food. Ever since he could remember, he had enjoyed thinking about things. Ryan had been one year old when the people at daycare had started calling him the "judge," and that name had stuck with him. His mom referred to his thinking as mind trips and said he was going to parts unknown. His grandmas encouraged these trips and said he was entertaining himself. He knew he wasn't just daydreaming because he was thinking about all kinds of stuff. He knew this helped him to remember things and it also helped him to figure things out when he had a problem. His grandma in Wyoming thought a mind trip was a great thinking tool and helped

Marcia Strausner

him to solve problems. She said problem solving was a skill he would need all of his life. Whatever it was he knew it was a part of him, and he liked it.

His mom repeated with emphasis on *Ryan*, "Earth to Ryan!" Ryan smiled at his mother, finished gobbling down his last bite of syrupy pancakes, and took his last gulp of orange juice. He wiped his mouth on his sleeve and kissed her with a quick swipe of her cheek. He said good-bye to his dad, gave him a quick hug, grabbed his backpack, and then reached down and gave his little brother a hug good-bye.

He felt his mom grab his shoulder and say, "Wait a minute, young man. Is your lunch in your backpack? Show me where it is. Also, I'm waiting to hear you say, thank you, Mom, for making my lunch. Yes?" Ryan nodded his head yes for thank you as his mom continued, "Is your note in your backpack?" She checked to make sure it was there, and then hearing the doorbell she finished with, "Aaron's here. Now give me a proper good-bye kiss before you go."

Ryan smiled and said, "Oh, Mom." He gave her a kiss on the cheek and headed for the door to greet Aaron, his next-door neighbor. As he was going out the door, he heard his dad yell, "I love you, Ryan; work hard today."

Learning is Cool in Ryan's School

Lea watched from the doorway as Aaron and Ryan turned and ran down the first four front steps. They continued toward the lawn by leaping past the fifth step and landing on the sidewalk below. The boys were two of a kind; both of them seemed to be moving continuously. It was impossible for either boy to be still. They

ran past the Japanese maple tree in the yard, and
Ryan reached out to touch its feathery green
and purple leaves. Lea smiled as she watched
him touch his favorite tree. Since he had been
a toddler, he had liked trees, but this tree was
special. She knew Ryan was curious about all
of nature, but trees had always had a special
place in his heart. At times he seemed to com-
municate with them. Sometimes his mom had
laughed about it, and other times she'd been
amazed and had wondered at his reaction to
this part of nature.

She continued to watch as the boys ran the
rest of the way to Tommy's house, their backpacks flopping on their backs. They jumped
over bushes and pretended to throw an invisi-
ble football and then to catch it. Tommy's front
step turned out to be the goal line. Aaron made
the touchdown. Aaron lived next door to Ryan,
and Tommy lived three houses away on the
other side of him. Tommy was waiting on his
steps. He wasn't about to walk any farther than
he had to. It was late, and he figured they'd
have to run the two blocks to school anyway.

Ryan and Aaron paused only long enough

to take a breath when they reached Tommy. Tommy stood up and yelled, "Race you—last one to Verda James loses." The boys laughed and started running toward their school. Tommy was the first to arrive because he'd been rested when they'd started running. Ryan said, between gasps for air, "Tommy, that's not fair; you cheated."

Tommy laughed and said, "Too bad for you and Aaron," and he ran into the building.

Tommy was hanging up his backpack when Aaron and Ryan walked down the hall to their classroom. Their parents had requested the same teacher because the three boys were friends and they played together. The boys had begged for this. The parents had met, discussed the pros and cons, and decided to try putting them together. However, they would be on probation. That meant they could stay in the same class as long as they finished their work on time, got good grades, tried their hardest, weren't disruptive in class, didn't talk too much, and about ten other behaviors they were not supposed to do. The most important condition concerned the teacher. If Mrs. Becker ever thought they needed to be separated, they would be moved to separate classes. The school had three sections of second grade and the boys knew there was room in the other classes for them. The parents had chosen Mrs. Becker as the teacher because she was thorough and structured in her teaching. Their kids would be sure to get the basics in her room. The boys were told if they wanted to stay together they had to obey all of her rules, and they needed to show Mrs. Becker they were learning. Most of the time, the boys behaved. It wasn't long before the friends loved their new teacher and wanted to please her because she was nice to them.

For her part Mrs. Becker assigned them to seats in different parts of the classroom. Ryan's desk was in the row nearest the door. Tommy sat in the middle row, and Aaron was seated across the room in the front seat. They weren't sitting together, but they were close enough for them to make eye contact.

Mrs. Becker taught some of the standards for second grade using computers. Usually the day began and ended with her students using them in some way. Ryan was always anxious to get the school day started because he had science and geography first. There were sixteen computers and twenty-four students in his class. Half of the class did science and geography at their seats, and half went to the computers. They switched when they had finished the seatwork or had completed the work on the computers.

The bell rang as Ryan and Aaron hung up their backpacks. The boys bolted into the classroom, nearly running into Heath and Halea, the redheaded twins who did not look alike. Mrs. Becker frowned at the boys, and the word *sorry* came out of their mouths as they sat down in their seats.

Today Ryan did seatwork first. While getting his writing book out, Ryan looked at the white board at the front of the room. He noticed the sentences said something about the weather. Now, reading more closely, he noticed the first sentence said, "All weather begins with the son." Ryan quickly corrected the sentence by writing, "All weather begins with the sun." Next he looked at the second sentence and read the words: "Twoday our humidity in the air is 100 percent." He corrected the sentence to: "Today our humidity in the air is 100 percent." Number three was: "If that were true, i would no because it would bee raining outside" Ryan corrected the sentence by capitalizing the first word in the sentence, changing the lower case *i* to a capital *I*, changing *bee* to *be*, and ending the sentence with a period. He decided he was glad it wasn't raining outside.

He closed his booklet and headed to the computer center to check the weather forecast for the day on one of the empty computers. He pulled the Web site up on the screen, and the map showed rain and clouds all down the east side of the U.S. He wondered why it wasn't raining in Atlanta. The temperature was going to be in the seventy-degree range. He certainly wouldn't need the jacket he kept in his backpack. Ryan also checked the weather for Wyoming to see if it was raining on his grandparents. It wasn't, and as he was getting ready to quit, he noticed the words "Gulf of Mexico" at the bottom of the map. That was one of the clues that Grandma had used last night about the spring break trip. There had been a clue about the gulf and one about a lot of rain. He noticed there were many states around the Gulf of Mexico. Grandma had said the state they would be visiting was the largest state in the contiguous U.S., and it was easy to see that was Texas.

The next part of his class assignment was to find and write down one state and its capital. Since he was already looking at Texas, he wrote its name down and looked for the city with a star by it. Mrs. Becker had taught them the star meant it was the capital. He found it in the southeastern part of the state, or maybe he should say the south central part. He copied the word *Austin* down. He knew his grandma had written another clue, but he couldn't remember what it was. His friend Zella was standing behind him, so he went to "File" at the top of the screen, clicked close to close his window, smiled at Zella, and said, "Your turn." And then he went back to his desk.

Mrs. Becker had been walking around the room helping students correct the sentences. She turned to the class and said, "Boys and girls, you have five minutes until we say the pledge and check our sentences and computer work. We will have a test over our sentences on Friday. Is there anyone who needs help?"

Mrs. Becker ended up standing behind Ryan's desk. She checked his sentences and said quietly, "Ryan, I think you should check sentence number three. Can you find your mistake?" Ryan reread his answer for number three and found his mistake. He changed *no* to *know.* He knew that was an easy mistake to make and that now he would get 100 percent on today's assignment.

The rest of the morning went really well because the class was busy. In reading they were still learning about weather. Their book was titled *What Makes Weather?* He'd known that water could freeze and thaw and that frozen water was ice. He put ice from his refrigerator in all his drinks because he liked his drinks really cold. However, he'd never thought about water changing to ice as a chemical reaction. He'd need to ask his dad about chemical reactions.

He was starving by recess and decided he would grab a cheese stick out of his lunch. He was glad his mom always added extra food in case he was hungry. If he didn't eat the extra food, it was okay. It was nice to have the choice. He'd have the cheese stick eaten by the time he made it to the playing fields.

The first kids out to the field chose the game all of them would play because everyone had to use the same field. The kids in rooms nearest the outside door usually were the first to the field. Ryan's room was at the end of the hall, so he was hardly ever first. Some kids chose to play football and some chose to play soccer.

Soccer season had started in February, and Ryan had already played several games. They'd won some and lost some. His parents said it didn't matter if they won or lost. They said learning the skills needed to play, being a good sport, and having fun were the most important things when you played sports. However, some of the other adults didn't act as if they really meant that. They yelled at the referees and told their kids what to do. Alex's dad even ran up and down the field yelling at him when he made a mistake and then telling Alex how to play. Ryan felt sorry for him. It would be embarrassing if his dad had done that. Aaron,

Ryan, and Tommy had talked about the pressure, and Tommy had chosen not to play. He said he'd rather do something no one could be mad at him for. At recess Tommy usually hung out with Josh. However, Ryan and Aaron, along with Jesse and Matt, enjoyed the competition. Sometimes they won, and sometimes they lost. Ryan knew for sure that winning was more fun. The boys usually joined in with the third graders and were happiest when they could play better than the older boys.

The afternoon seemed to drag on. Math was not Ryan's favorite thing, and he had a hard time concentrating on the dreaded multiplication facts. The whole class was learning them, and the students had learned up to the fours. Ryan's dad had shown him some multiplication tricks like doubling the twos for the fours and the crazy nines. However, his mom had said, "Ryan, you're ahead of the game if you just memorize them. The faster you learn them, the better it will be for you because you have to know them forever. You can then use the tricks to help with the ones you forget."

His grandma said that if he could add he

could multiply, that multiplication was just repeated addition. Then she had said that if you could multiply you could divide and division was a way of subtracting and grouping numbers. Ryan could hardly believe it could be that easy. He was trying, but the multiplication facts were difficult for him, and his teacher hadn't introduced division. He and his mom practiced the facts at the dinner table at night.

When math was finally over, Mr. Vasques, his Spanish teacher, came into the room. Ryan had been learning the Spanish language since he'd started kindergarten. He'd learned words like *papá* for *daddy, mamá* for *mama, hermano* for *brother* and *hermana* for the word *sister.* His favorite songs that year were "Feliz Navidad" and "Jingle Bells." He could remember all the words to them. In first grade he'd learned more words like *perro* for *dog, gato* for *cat,* and some school words, like pencil, he couldn't remember. This year he'd learned the colors, that *baño* was bathroom, *agua* was water, and *feliz cumpleaños* meant happy birthday. Today Mr. Vasques taught the class a song about Easter called "Hidden Eggs for Easter." The words were sung to the tune of "The Wheels on the Bus," and the words were:

The eggs in the basket
Are hidden,
Are hidden,
Are hidden.
The eggs in the basket are hidden,
Hidden in the yard.

In Spanish the song went:

Los huevos en la cesta
Están escondidos,
Están escondidos,
Eastán escondidos.
Los huevos en la cesta
Están escondidos,
Escondidos en el patio.

The song "The Wheels on the Bus" had been a favorite of Ryan's since he was a baby because it was one of the very first songs he'd learned. Today the Spanish version was pretty fun because they made up several verses of the song about where they would hide the eggs.

Ryan ended the day with more computer work. He had his own e-mail address, and he was required to send one message per day. He was supposed to use his typing skills and to write at least three sentences. He preferred to use the hunt-and-peck method to type the words. However, he did intend to learn his keyoarding skills because he wanted to type as fast as his mother could type. Her fingers seemed to fly over the keys. He thought she probably held some kind of record for typing fast, and she had short fingers like Ryan. If she could do it, so could he.

Ryan decided to write to his grandma in Wyoming because he needed to answer her message from last night. When he checked his school e-mail, he found he had a message from his dad, so he quickly replied. His dad's message said,

Dear Ryan, I hope you are having fun in school today. Are you? I think about you a lot. Love, Dad.

Ryan replied,

> Dear Dad, I made a goal in soccer at recess, I'm hungry, and what is a chemical reaction? Love, Ryan.

That message took so long that Ryan decided to go straight to sustained silent reading and to skip writing to his grandma.

On his way to his desk, Ryan checked on Tommy by poking him in the back. Tommy was reading a book on science experiments to get ideas for the primary science fair that was coming up after Easter vacation. It looked interesting, so Ryan asked him if he could read it next. He noticed Mrs. Becker was watching him so he returned to his seat, pulled his book out of his desk, found his bookmark, opened his book, and began to read. The book was about freshwater animals. He was on page twenty-nine, and it had pictures of carnivorous fish. He knew *carnivorous* meant they ate other animals. That was cool. The page also showed where these fish lived. He read that trout lived in clear running water. He had caught a trout when he was fishing with his grandpa in Wyoming. He even got to eat it. However, he had not been a fan of taking the hook out of that wiggling fish. For now his grandpa said he would take his hooks out. As Ryan was thinking about fishing in Wyoming with his grandpa, the bell rang. The class put their books away, put their chairs on their desks, and waited for Mrs. Becker to dismiss them.

Mrs. Becker dismissed her students and then reminded them she had scheduled a study session for those students who wanted to stay and work on the multiplication facts. Ryan, Tommy, and Aaron checked with each other across the room and decided they'd had enough school for the day. Only four kids, Trista, Leah, Kylee, and Barbara, waited in the room while the rest of the class walked to the hall. The boys had wanted to get out of the classroom door first, but they knew Mrs. Becker would make them go back to their desks and start over if they ran. They had learned it was better to walk out of the room the first time from experience. The boys walked until they reached the outside door of the school. They gave it a great push and rushed out as if they'd been cooped up for a year in a tiny space. They were free!

Grandchildren
Solve the Riddle

The parents of the three boys had set up the after-school rules for safety reasons. The boys had been coached, drilled, and quizzed about those rules. Rule number one was: you must stay together when walking home. No excuses accepted. Number two was: always use the crosswalks. You know why. Three: if you are not home thirty minutes after school is out, a parent will come looking for you.

The boys learned they meant it the day Aaron's grandma had come looking for them. They had been in big trouble. None of the rules were hard for the boys except this last one. They found so many interesting things going on in the neighborhood, and there were so many games to play; it was hard for them to come straight home from school. However, the parents had no sympathy for them. Each kid was responsible for communicating with his parents. As soon as the last bell had rung at Verda James Elementary School, the rules applied.

All of the boys' parents worked. Ryan's mom was an attorney who worked from home, but she had meetings all over the city of Atlanta. Aaron's mom was an instructor in a community college, and Tommy's mom sold books at elementary school book fairs. They all took turns being home after school. It was difficult to arrange individual schedules to fit that time, but grandparents and older brothers and sisters helped out. Everyone agreed it took a neighborhood to take care of its children. Today they were going to Ryan's house.

As the boys reached the crosswalk in front of school, they looked for Duran, their high-school friend. Duran was a volunteer crosswalk guard. He worked once a week. He had gone to school at Verda, and now he volunteered at his old school. The boys liked him because he was nice and they knew he was the state single's tennis champ at his high school. Ryan knew him because he had been a coach at Ryan's summer tennis camp. As usual, Duran was helping some first graders cross the busy street. As the boys waited their turn to cross, Ryan thought he might help little kids when he got into high school.

Duran saw them and said, "Hi, guys, how was school today? Been playing any tennis, Ryan?"

Ryan smiled and answered, "No tennis, just playing soccer now. I will play tennis this summer."

Duran answered with, "See you next week."

The boys walked across the street and started to race down the next block. They stopped running when they were gasping for air. The boys decided they couldn't breathe because they were starving to death. They knew a snack was waiting for them at Ryan's house. The kids sprinted the rest of the distance to Ryan's house and food.

Ryan gave his mom a quick hug as the boys ran through the front door. Brady came running down the hall gleeful that his brother was home at last. Tommy and Aaron grabbed Brady and tossed him on the couch. Brady giggled, crawled off the couch, and said, "Again." The big boys ignored him and headed for the kitchen and family room.

While they were eating, Ryan's mom asked the boys questions about their day. She had learned to ask specific questions because if she asked, "How was your day?" Ryan would simply say, "Okay." By playing Twenty Questions, she learned the details that were so important to a mom.

Aaron finished eating first and wanted another sandwich. Tommy finished next; then Brady finished, and Ryan finished last because he'd answered his mom's questions. Between bites he asked his mom, "Did you talk to Grandma today?"

She answered, "Yes, Ryan, and she sent you an e-mail with the next clues in it. When the boys go home, I'll check it with you."

Since they had no homework, Lea sent them to the basement to play. The boys raced down the stairs, tripping over each other. It was a good thing Albert, Ryan's dad, wasn't home. If the noise hadn't killed him the *accident waiting to happen* would've. Basketballs, footballs, and soccer balls soon were flying around the room as a game of free-for-all dodge ball began. Much to his dismay, Lea had kept Brady upstairs because as Lea said, "Honey, those big boys are too rough for you. You will get hurt. I'm sorry."

The phone soon began ringing, and Tommy went home to his older sister, Kristin, and Aaron went home to his dad because Aaron's mom had a meeting at school and his older sister Megan had play practice.

Ryan and his mom headed for their computer as soon as Aaron left. It was located in the family office in the front of the house. This office was where his mom did most of her job. There were two computers and two lines for

DESTINATION SAN ANTONIO, TX

the Internet. Ryan had spent a lot of time in that office with her and had learned a lot about computers. He could access his e-mail account and download pictures into the picture gallery from their digital camera. It took only minutes until he had accessed his message from his grandma. It said,

> To Whom It May Concern:
> (That's you, my grandchildren),
> Hear ye, Hear ye, can you hear it?
> A message for you,
> A clue to our great adventure
> Our destination is famous
> for its history.
> Behold the city!
> A river runs through it.
> You know the state
> Now name the city.
> Two words = five syllables
> Do you have the will to do it?
> The journey will make
> This destination better.
> Where, oh where, are we going?
> Love, Grandma

As Ryan got his map book of states from the bookcase, he told his mom about the Gulf of Mexico and how he thought the state was Texas but he hadn't had time to look for the city. Opening the page to the state of Texas didn't take long because the *T* was easy to find. Ryan couldn't remember all the clues Grandma had given in her first riddle, so they looked them up. Now it was easy to see that Texas was the state, and knowing the city was 140 miles from the gulf was a really good clue. It took only another few minutes to decide the destination was San Antonio, Texas. They knew for sure when they clapped out the syllables for San Antonio and found there were five claps.

Ryan clicked on Reply and typed,

Dear Grandma, one of your grandchildren from GA says we are going to San Antonio, Texas. Yea! Why are we going there?

Love, Ryan

He clicked on Send, and it was on its way.

On the other side of the United States, Ryan's cousin Daniel hurried into his house after school. He'd waited all day for this time to come, and he had it all planned out. First he would get a yogurt and a glass of apple juice for his hungry stomach, and then he'd go straight to "Daniel's Den." Anna was with him, but he hardly noticed her. Today both kids were scheduled to practice their music lessons. Anna practiced the piano in the living room, and Daniel had his den. His den was his special place.

Daniel loved music. He liked all kinds of music, but he especially liked guitar and drum music. There wasn't a musical instrument that he didn't want to learn to play. When he was five, his grandpa had given him his old trombone, and everyone had discovered Daniel had a good lip. His dad played the trumpet for church, so Daniel knew how important a good lip was in order to play a brass instrument. His grandparents had also bought him a drum set, much to his parents' displeasure. His mom had given him his grandma's old guitar, and he'd strummed on that guitar until he'd been given one more his size. He'd started taking lessons in the third grade from Mrs. Stein, and everyone said he had a knack for it. He often pretended he was playing for crowds of people and he could hear the crowds cheering and singing the words to his songs.

His playing drove his parents crazy until his dad had done a most wonderful thing. They had a playroom/guestroom in the front of their house, and off that room was a large walk-in closet. The closet had always been filled with old clothes, blankets, shoes, and coats. They hardly ever used any of it. His mom had cleared all the stuff out of the room and had made several trips to Goodwill. His dad had taken out the rods they'd hung clothes on and sound proofed the walls with special padding. He put a new yellow carpet on the floor and a solid door. There was a window on the back wall so Daniel would have plenty of air. It turned out to be a nice-sized room because there was space for his trap drum set, his guitar, his trombone, the keyboard his grandparents had given to both him and Anna, and a microphone setup. When it was all done, his parents had given him a sign that said "Daniel's Den." Then his dad nailed it to the top of the doorframe.

Daniel had been so thrilled with *his* room he could hardly talk about it. He used the room for many things. Besides practicing the drums and guitar, he used it for a clubhouse when his friends came over, he used it to listen to his CD player, he used it to get away from Anna, and he used it to cool down when he was angry. Daniel had a bad temper, and his mom often sent him to his den to cool off. He cooled off by playing his drums as hard and as loudly as he wanted. He could play to his heart's content because the room was sound proof.

This afternoon he wanted to practice his new music on the guitar. Mrs. Stein had introduced it during his last lesson, and it was hard. He knew he'd get it in time. He just needed to practice.

Shutting himself in his den, he began to play. He warmed up with the drums and then worked on his guitar music. He didn't know how much time went by, but a pounding on his door got his attention. He opened his door, and it was his mom. She told him dinner would be ready in ten minutes so he should finish up. Daniel smiled at how good he felt, cleaned up the already clean room, and headed for the bathroom. He arrived at the dinner table a little early.

Daniel could hear piano music coming from the living room. Anna was still playing. He would earn points with his mom because he'd come right away.

His mom stood in the kitchen door and raised her voice as she said, "Anna, it's time; come now!" Anna had been singing as she was playing. She had a good voice and had taken some singing lessons. She had been singing solos in choirs since she was six years old. Anna stopped playing and walked into the kitchen. She looked at Daniel and said, "I sure wish I had a special room to sing and play in. Mom and Dad, when do I get my special room?"

Her parents looked at each other, and her dad said, "Anna, haven't we been through this discussion before? Have you even decided what kind of room you want?"

She looked down as she answered, "No, but it's still not fair for Daniel to have his den and I have nothing."

Her mom smiled and answered her by saying, "Well, Anna, all you have to do is decide, and Dad and I will see what we can do. Until you decide, I suggest you quit complaining."

Not wanting to give up on this argument, Anna mumbled, "I don't know where we'd put it if I did think of something."

Dad intervened as he said, "Let's ask the blessing so we can eat. Lynn, will you say grace?"

There was much conversation and some laughing as they ate their meal of spaghetti and meatballs. Daniel answered questions about the music he was playing, and Anna wanted to talk about the mysterious trip. Mom wanted to talk about a friend who was having family troubles, and Dad talked about the next trip he would take for his job. There was to be more testing done for his company. He would need to go back to Florida. There seemed to be plenty to talk about, and no one was left out of the conversation.

Each member of the family helped to clear the table while dad put the dishes in the dishwasher. Then each person went on to the next chore. The kids did their homework with Zoey helping them by giving them sloppy kisses. Dad walked the ten steps to the office to check the mail, and their mom studied for the class she taught to a group of high-school girls at church.

Next came phone calls, putting homework into backpacks, and Daniel answering his e-mail message from Grandma. Anna and his mom helped him decide the destination really was San Antonio and, like Ryan, they knew for sure when they counted the syllables in San Antonio. Daniel was glad when he clicked "Send" and he could go upstairs to shower before bed. In his wildest dreams he never thought he'd be glad to take a shower. He had worked up a sweat playing the drums.

Dear Kids,
Yea! The destination has been discovered.
The journey is under way.
Ryan asked the question, "why?
Why San Antonio, Grandma, why?"
To help you answer the question,
I've included a recipe for a successful trip.
Tonight I need you to check the ingredients.
Do we have them all?
Or do we need to work on a few?
Your answers are up to you.
This is your assignment to complete.
The answers will help us when we meet.

Grandma's Recipe for a Successful Trip

The next day the cousins received this e-mail message from Wyoming.

Dear Kids, Yea! The destination has been discovered. The journey is under way. Ryan asked the question, "Why? Why San Antonio, Grandma, why?"

To help you answer the question, I've included a recipe for a successful trip. Tonight I need you to check the ingredients. Do we have them all? Or do we need to work on a few? Your answers are up to you. This is your assignment to complete. The answers will help us when we meet. A Recipe for a Successful Trip Developed and written by Grandma with input from Grandpa:

Ingredients:

1. Three grandchildren—Anna, Daniel, and Ryan
2. One grandma—Grandma Jean
3. Destination—San Antonio, Texas
4. Money for the basic needs—food, shelter, clothing, money for transportation, and money for entertainment
5. Time—five days if you count Thursday, plus four nights
6. Umbrella Plan—gives structure, caters to interests of the participants, must include wiggle room.

Ryan is interested in nature and all kinds of marine life. He likes all rides and doesn't get sick.

Daniel loves the rides in theme parks and doesn't get motion sick. He likes science, nature, and music.

Anna likes shopping in malls for clothes and cool jewelry. She likes listening to music, and she likes warm weather. She also likes science, nature, and theme parks.

Grandma likes pretty scenery with green somewhere in it; she likes learning history and being with her family and grandkids, and she likes warm weather. She likes nature, science, and likes to ride rides in theme parks. She doesn't get motion sick.

Add:

1. A touch of patience
2. Some sleep
3. Some cooperation
4. Some kindness

Include:

1. Some adventure
2. A chance to learn something new
3. Some physical activity

Stir ingredients together. Watch as the trip to San Antonio, Texas, turns into a smashing success and watch as *mountains become molehills* in our journey.

P.S. Please print a copy of this recipe for each of you. You will use the copy as a guide when you prepare for our trip.

P.P.S. Put a checkmark by each part of the recipe we already have. Put a circle by the parts we need to work on. Put a question mark by the parts you don't understand.

Think about this:

When does our journey end? Does it end when we reach our destination? How does our journey make our destination better? I'm giving you time to think about these questions. I will ask for your answers later.

Love, Grandma

Ryan answered first. His message said:

Dear Grandma,

My mom and I worked on this part of the journey together. She is also typing this because she is fast and I am slow. There is a lot to type tonight. I know you said to think about the questions, but I already know what my answer will be. I think this journey will be over when I get back home. Mom thinks this journey will never end because the experience will become a part of me. My answer is easier. Now about the recipe, I put checks by the ingredients 1, 2, 3, and 5. I put circles by the numbers 4 and 6 and the "Add" and the "Include" parts. I put a question mark by the basic needs. What does that mean? I also don't understand what an "Umbrella Plan" is, and what is wiggle room? Good night.

Love, Ryan

P.S. This sounds like a pretty good recipe. I wonder how it will taste. Ha ha.

Grandma received Daniel's reply next. It said:

Dear Grandma,

Anna and I called a family meeting, and we all talked about your recipe. Anna and I disagreed on some things, so these are *my* answers. I put a check mark by 1, 2, 3, 4, (I have lots of money we can use) and number 5. Under "Add," I put a check by sleep and kindness, but why do we need patience and cooperation? I put a question mark by them. I also don't understand an "Umbrella Plan," so we need to work on that. We also need to work on the "Include" part. Good night.

Love, Daniel

P.S. I'm thinking about your questions.

Anna's message came shortly after Daniel's. Her answer began:

Dear Grandma,

I know what you're doing. You're trying to see if we have the will to do the planning for our adventure and to make us think about the trip. You think this is part of the journey, don't you? You are sneaky. It's working. The whole family has gotten involved because Daniel and I called a family meeting tonight. We talked about this recipe of yours. Mom and Daddy mostly asked questions like, what does she mean when she says an "Umbrella Plan" and do you think she made up the recipe or did she copy it from somewhere? I told them I was sure you made it up. You did, didn't you?

I know Daniel has already sent you his answers. We have some answers the same, but some are different. I think we already have the ingredients 1, 2, 3, and 5. I think we have some of 4, but it could use some work. I think I understand we've already learned something new for the "Include" part but need to work on adventure and physical activity.

What I don't understand is the "Umbrella Plan" part. We already know Ryan likes fish, that Daniel likes rides, that I like to shop, and that you like history and scenery, but what does that have to do with our trip? I think we should have a plan, but what does an umbrella have to do with it? You said it rains a lot in San Antonio. Is this a plan in case it rains?

I've also thought about our bonus questions. I think there could be two answers. I think the journey could end at the destination because you said the journey makes the destination better; or the journey could end when we get home. I'm too tired to decide now. Wouldn't it be fun to travel all the time? Life could be one long journey. Good night.

Love, Anna

After reading the messages, Grandma leaned back in her rolling black office chair and smiled. The grandchildren were getting into the spirit of things. Her sister Sam couldn't believe that she would take three children on a five day trip by herself, and her husband had even voiced some reservations. She smiled to herself again as she thought about Grandpa. He knew the reasons she had decided to do this trip. Spending time together would help the cousins' relationships, and it would be a chance to get to know her grandkids better without parental involvement. She would also see them under some unusual circumstances. Of course she had questions about what to do to keep three active kids busy and learning. Yes, this was going to be an adventure but one that would be worth all the money and planning. The family had been through some good times and some tough times. She was thankful for both because adversity needed to be balanced with happy times. Both made healthy people who were survivors. Healthy people made healthy families. Now, before she would go to sleep she would answer the kids' e-mails.

She wrote:

My dear grandchildren,

I'm writing to you tonight because I wanted you to know you made me proud today when you answered my message. All of you are absolutely brilliant, of course. I loved that you followed directions, that you asked your parents for help, and that you got caught up in the moment. I thought you asked excellent questions and appreciated your prompt answers.

In the next days we will continue to explore our "Recipe for a Successful Trip," but tonight I want to address the "Umbrella Plan." I expected all of you to have questions about it, and you did. Now, I want you to picture an umbrella in your mind. Think about how it's made and what it is used for. You might even think in color. What does your umbrella look like? The umbrella in my mind is red with a black handle. There's a red strap on the handle. When it's open it's shaped like a dome. There are strong metal spokes to support the dome. These spokes collapse easily when I close it. My umbrella has many uses. It helps me feel prepared for the weather and then protects me from the sun, wind, and rain when I open it. I can also choose whether I use it or not. It helps me to stay organized because I have to keep track of it. Now think about our trip. Organization and planning will help us to enjoy San Antonio better. A plan will protect us from being bored and will keep us from wasting time while we decide what to do. In other words we will all know what to expect, and in turn, what will be expected of us. Our plan will help us to be better prepared for our activities. Like our umbrellas, we can choose when to use our plan. We can also choose not to use it if circumstances won't allow us the time, energy, or desire to do an activity. This is wiggle room, Ryan. Wiggle room means we don't have to stick to the plan if we don't want to. So, my dear children, our "Umbrella Plan" will be used as a guide and will protect us from sad feelings, exhaustion, and mountains caused by lack of time and lack of communication.

Since we had to spend so much time on the trip today, you will not have any questions to answer or jobs to do tomorrow. Good night and love back to you,

Your Grandma

The Recipe and a Side Dish

The next day Grandma was scheduled to be a judge at her school's primary science fair. She took a walk along the creek before she left for the school. She thought about the adventure she was about to have with her grandchildren. Then she thought about all the things that could go wrong on the trip. She knew she was worrying about things that probably would not happen, but the old adage about *an ounce of prevention being better than a pound of cure* seemed to stick in her mind. For her peace of mind, she felt she *could leave no stone unturned* as she prepared for this very important trip. She finished her walk, and then she wrote this message and sent it off to the kids.

To Whom It May Concern:

The Parable of Wasted Time

One day four people decided to take a trip. They wanted to go for three reasons. They wanted to spend some time together. They wanted to have fun, and they wanted to learn a few things. Their destination was in a rainy far country. With haste, they proceeded to their destination. Sure enough, it began raining as soon as they reached their shelter. It rained indecision when three of the people needed food for survival and one did not like the food available and would not eat it. Oh, it rained! It rained selfishness and discontent. Three people decided if one person could have his or her way, each one of them should have the same privilege. So the first night was spent eating snacks in the shelter because making the decision of where to eat was deemed impossible. Two people went swimming in the shelter's pool, and two people watched television. They didn't learn much, didn't have much fun, and didn't much like each other. One person thought they had come to a far land to disagree. This was not fun! They all felt frustrated and wondered if this trip would be a waste of time.

Each day brought more rain because that's how humans are made. Humans can be very selfish. They want things to go their way. They want everything to be exactly the way they think it should be. Each person thinks he or she knows what is best. And what's more, he or she knows that on more than one occasion his or her way has been proven to be the best way for others. Each person thinks the rest of the group should know this and should act accordingly. Some of the people even called this attitude "leadership."

The rains continued for the next days, and the rains turned from discontent to dissatisfaction with the trip until a rain of *let's just get through this the best we can* came. That rain helped some, but it was almost time to return home. After all, the trip had gotten off to a bad start, and there are just some things you can't forgive and forget. Being unappreciated is one of those things.

And so the travelers returned home. They had spent time together. They'd had some fun. And they had learned some things about a far country. Alas, no one was satisfied. No one was truly happy with the trip, not even the person who had insisted that everything had to be done the way he or she wanted. The rains hadn't stopped the trip, but they had impacted the quality of the time they had spent together. They had needed an umbrella to protect them from those rains. Yea for umbrellas!

Love from your Grandma

There was no work on the trip that night, but the parable was discussed in both homes. Does Grandma think I'm selfish? Who is she talking about? Questions like these were discussed until both sets of parents reminded their children that parables are supposed to teach you something and obviously Grandma didn't want anyone to be selfish or to spoil the trip. The ball was in the kids' court.

The next day brought another message from Grandma. It said,

My Dear Grandchildren,

I wrote the *Parable of Wasted Time* yesterday because I was trying to solve problems before they occurred. I know that all of us enjoy being the boss, and I know you've heard that *too many chief cooks can spoil the broth.* We can now move on, knowing each of us will take care not to be the bossy or selfish one on our trip. Before we begin planning, we need to see how far we've journeyed. I looked at your answers to the recipe again, and I will summarize what I think you said. If I made a mistake about your answers, please let me know.

You all agreed that we already have the grandchildren, grandma, and the destination ingredients for our trip. You also agree that we have the time scheduled. Anna and Ryan are concerned about money for the trip and think we need to work on that. Daniel has saved money and is willing to spend it on the trip. You all think we need to understand and work on the "Umbrella Plan," the "Add" part, and the "Include" part.

As the adult and the one paying for your airline tickets, food, and hotel room, I made up the "Umbrella Plan" as a guide to ensure that yesterday's parable would not happen to us. Ryan, you asked what "basic needs" were. All people need food and water, shelter, and clothing (to protect from the elements). These are the basic needs for life. You will probably learn this in second grade.

To ensure that each of us will get to do something that is of special interest, we will follow our "Umbrella Guide." We will have no Cinderellas on this trip. By planning with our individual interests in mind, we can all benefit when we share in the activities. In other words, we will all enjoy going to Sea World with Ryan. I looked at the available activities, and Sea World has the most to offer when it comes to marine life. Is going to Sea World okay with you, Ryan?

Next, we know how much Daniel likes to ride the rides at an amusement park. How do you feel about going to Six Flags Fiesta Texas, Daniel? The information pamphlet says there are super thrill rides. Are you up for that?

And for you, Anna, we know how much you like to shop. It just so happens there is a wonderful mall on the River Walk that has all the stores you like. Yea! The boys can shop for souvenirs while you shop for clothes. I have coupons to help us with the cost, so we are set, if you approve.

And for your grandma, San Antonio is full of history and beautiful scenery. You will love floating down the river that flows through San Antonio and will learn a lot about Texas history. I know you've heard about the Battle of the Alamo, but do you know there were women and children there too? Do you know what the words "Remember the Alamo!" meant to the history of Texas? Well, you will find out. We will begin our history lesson at the IMAX Theatre located in Anna's mall.

Ryan asked me why we were going to San Antonio. Now you know. San Antonio, Texas, offers all the things we like to do! There's something for each of us. San Antonio has been called the Alamo City, City in the Sun, and the Cradle of Texas Liberty. I read in Conrad Stien's children's book, "All Texans have two home towns, the one they are living in and San Antonio. San Antonio is a Texan's heart, soul, and its roots." I also learned that San Antonio was the territorial capital of the countries of Spain and Mexico. Franciscan missionaries founded the Mission San Antonio De Valero in 1718. That's over two hundred eighty years ago! The city was also called San Antonio de Bexar at the time of the Battle of the Alamo. The Battle of the Alamo occurred in March of 1836. That's almost 170 years ago. Yes, Anna, I did round off those numbers. I knew you'd check. You go, girl!

I will let you decide when we should do

our activities, and then I will make our reservations. I have some coupons that will help with the cost. Your part of the money will be the amount you want for your spending money. You may bring as much or as little money as you like. However, you will be responsible for your money. If you lose your money, it's gone. Of course, we would be sad if you lost it, but I will not replace lost money because you are the ones who need to be responsible.

Tonight I'd like for you to find the distance to San Antonio from your cities and to think about what day and time you want to visit Sea World, Six Flags, and the mall. I want you to think about what clothes you'd like to wear and if you will be bringing a camera or video games. Our hotel has a swimming pool, so we will be able to swim there. Decide which suitcase you will bring. You will check that at the airport. Please bring your backpacks as your carry-on. Your backpacks should carry your necessities, whatever you decide they are. You will be responsible for a water bottle, cameras, games, books, or whatever else you bring. I will not carry your things. One more time, *you* are responsible for your stuff. If you decide to bring a lot of things, your suitcase and backpack will be very heavy. That's okay, but you will be carrying it. Please e-mail me what you will be carrying in your backpack so I will have some idea what you plan to do on the airplane. We will also take our backpacks with us when we are traveling around San Antonio. Wow, there's so much preparation and so little time. San Antonio, here we come. Yea!

Grandma

P.S. I almost forgot. The weekend we are in San Antonio has been designated as "Family Weekend along the River Walk." The scheduled activities include a talent show at the Arneson Theatre on Saturday night. This talent show is just for kids. I wondered if you would like to participate. Ryan, you could play the piano or drums. Anna, you could sing and play the piano, and Daniel, you could bring the crowd down with your drums or guitar. If you had time to practice, maybe you could play together in The Cousins' Band. We could rent instruments there. Oh dear, I'm full of ideas, but it will be up to you individually whether you participate or not. See you soon. Are we on our journey yet?

Love from your Grandma

The next days were filled with planning, packing and repacking, and last -minute questions. Should we bring film for our cameras or buy it when we get there? Will we be cold on the airplane? Will there be terrorists on the airplane? How are we going to sleep in the hotel? Do we need to bring money for food on the airplane? Do we need to bring dress-up clothes? Do we need to bring homework? Should we bring a book to read? Grandma answered some of the questions like how they would sleep in the hotel. They would stay in a double room; and she and Anna would sleep together, and Daniel and Ryan would share the other queen-sized bed. However, the kids figured out the rest of the answers.

The kids decided they would go to Sea World on Friday morning. They decided they would spend time on the River Walk Friday night and would take a boat ride on the river. They all had decided to participate in the talent show on Saturday night and decided they would check out the Arneson Theatre while they were touring on Friday night. Grandma would make the arrangements to rent a piano or keyboard for Anna. Ryan would need a set of drums, and Daniel needed an electric guitar. Saturday morning would be spent watching the IMAX movie and practicing for the talent show. The afternoon would be spent shopping at the Riverwalk Mall, and they would finish getting ready for the talent show. They would tour the Alamo Sunday morning and go to Six Flags Fiesta Texas afterwards. On Monday they would spend more time on the River Walk and hang out until it was time to go to the airport on the shuttle.

The kids used the "Recipe for a Successful Trip" as a guide, and they worked hard not to be the person described in "The Parable of Wasted Time."

At last the questions were answered, and the luggage and backpacks were packed. That is when the parents started to react. There was so much stress going around you could feel it and hear it in their voices. What could be done to help the poor parents? Grandma had arrived at Ryan's house a few days earlier so she could play with Brady while his mom taught a training session. There were times grandma thought the parents might call off the trip. Grandma and the kids were excited, but the parents were struggling. This trip concerned their children, and they were not in control. Grandma sent an e-mail to California and insisted Lea and Al read it in Georgia. It said:

Please be happy for this grandma and her grandchildren. We have shown our will in our preparations and planning.

You have copies of our itinerary, so you will know where we are at all times. We will practice safety first in all things. Besides, God will be taking care of us as he always does.

Love from the grandma

She ended with:

The San Antonio National Airport is located in north central San Antonio, approximately eight miles or fifteen minutes from the downtown central business district. It has two terminals. Remember, Anna, you and Daniel will fly into terminal number one. Ryan and I will be there to meet you. Remember you can always call on your cell phone. I can't wait. When is the end of our journey? See you soon!

Flying, Time Travel, and the Avoidance of Predators

The next afternoon Lynn watched as Anna and Daniel entered Gate Four on Concourse B at the LAX Airport. Her eyes never left them as the kids proceeded down the jet way to board the airplane. They had passed through security easily, and the airline personnel had been informed the kids would be flying without parents. The airlines had assured the kids' mother of their safety. The plan was for an attendant to help them get seated and then escort them off the plane at the conclusion of the flight. Someone from the airlines would stay with Anna and Daniel until their grandma picked them up at Gate Six on Concourse A in San Antonio. Lynn fought back the tears that formed in her eyes.

As she stood watching the rest of the passengers board the plane, unwelcome thoughts seemed to flood her mind. Yes, Anna and Daniel were growing up, but there were times she wished they were still her babies. She thought this whole trip was a horrible idea. She'd tried to prepare them for the things that could happen on the trip. She'd told them how to open the door to the tiny bathroom in the airplane and then how to slide the knob to lock it. She'd instructed them to stand guard for each other outside the bathroom door and said they were absolutely not to go to the bathroom alone. She'd told them not to get out of their seats until the pilot announced it was okay to do so. The same instructions went for playing video games. They were not to play the games until a flight attendant or the pilot said it was okay. She'd told them to check for the exits on the airplane. She'd even told them about the tray tables and where to turn on the overhead lights and how to ask an attendant for help. She'd warned them one more time to watch for people who preyed on children. They were called predators for a reason. She'd tried to cover all the bases. Now they were gone, and she could not help them any more. They were on their own.

She remembered her mom saying all a parent could do was to prepare a child for any eventuality and the rest was up to the kid. Parenting was so hard. She had to let Anna and Daniel grow up. This trip would be good for them. She knew they'd have new experiences and would come back different because of those experiences. Lynn whispered once again, "Dear God, please keep them safe and bring them back to me."

She looked one last time at the now closed door to the jet way and turned to walk back to the parking garage. She'd planned a busy day so she could keep her mind busy. She knew herself well enough to know she could make herself a wreck over this trip. She could dwell on the what-ifs, or she could do the healthy thing and stay busy. She figured Grandma and Ryan had been flying for an hour and would land in plenty of time to meet Anna and Daniel's plane. Her children would be calling after they'd landed. She knew the kids were scheduled to land in two and a half hours, and she wouldn't be satisfied until that all-important call came. Until then she'd complete her scheduled activities.

Meanwhile, a flight attendant standing at the door of the airplane smiled at the kids and welcomed them aboard as they came through the door. She smiled again as she checked her list and asked a male attendant to help the kids find their seats. His name was Zack, and his smiling face seemed friendly enough. He asked the kids' names and how old they were. Then Zack hurried to get them settled and told them he would check on them later. They were assigned to a row of three seats. Daniel had the window seat and Anna had the middle seat. Anna wondered who would sit in the aisle seat.

Anna and Daniel stowed their backpacks under the seats in front of them. They buckled up with the seat belts and felt ready for the 727 airplane to take off. Settled, Daniel looked around the huge plane, following his mom's instructions. He checked the people who were sitting around them and checked for the nearest exits. It was then he noticed a man sitting two rows up. He was in the middle row and to their right. He was also looking around the plane, and he smiled when he saw Daniel looking at him. Daniel quickly looked down and then sneaked another look. Now the man was looking at Anna. Daniel quickly looked away, and then his eyes returned to look one more time. That man was staring at his sister! Could he be one of those predators they'd been warned about? Daniel knew one thing. No predator would get him or Anna! He thought about the poem he had read when he was learning about child molesters. It went something like, "Predator, predator, you may be lurking, but it's not working. I'm too smart for you." Well he'd be on the watch. Anna was already reading her book. She sure wasn't any protection for him.

It was then he remembered he needed something to do. He couldn't believe he'd forgotten that part. There was too much to remember. He unbuckled his seat belt and pulled out his backpack from under the seat in front of him. He unzipped it and pulled out the plastic bag of chocolate-chip cookies made with candy-coated chocolate. They were his favorite kind of cookie, and his mom had made them that morning. He ate one of his yummy-tasting cookies and took out *Chocolate Fever,* the book he was reading. He'd brought three books. The others were *Cowpokes and Desperadoes* and *The Island of the Blue Dolphins.* The cowboy book was really easy to read, but he'd decided to read it again because his dad had always wanted to be a cowboy. He and Daniel's uncle Paul had taken their families to the World Agricultural Expo in Tulare, California, for as many years as Daniel could remember. The families had a great time climbing in and out of the huge tractors and checking out the latest and best of the farm equipment. The brothers grew gardens in their backyards every year and insisted one never knew when a threshing machine or a huge combine would come in handy. The brothers hoped that maybe their sons would be farmers. However, Daniel figured he wouldn't grow up to be a cowboy. Probably he would have his own Christian rock band.

He looked up to see Anna watching him. He grinned and said, "Want a bite?" She shook her head no and then reminded Daniel to get his seatbelt buckled again.

No one had set in the aisle seat. Anna figured that was a good thing because the empty seat would give them more space in which to move around. It seemed to her the plane looked bigger from the outside and smaller from the inside than she'd remembered. They had flown to Wyoming three Christmases ago and once during a summer vacation, but she hadn't paid much attention because they'd been with their parents. She'd known her mom or dad would take care of any needs she'd had.

Anna looked out the window, checked one last time to see if her little brother was set for takeoff, and once again opened the book Mrs. Heisner, the school librarian, had suggested she read. Mrs. Heisner knew the kind of books her students liked to read. She knew Anna was interested in time travel, and this book was one of a series she had ordered for the library. The title was *Friends for All Time.* This was the second book she'd read in the series. The books were about five friends who traveled back in time. They were teenagers, and their names were Kelsey, Jessica, Abby, Becca, and Robyn. They traveled to meet and to learn about famous women in history. These young women wanted to know the characteristics of famous women because they intended to be famous.

In this book the girls were going to learn about the pilot, Amelia Earhart. Anna didn't know much about her and wondered if she was interesting and worth reading about. In the first book, Anna had learned about Eleanor Roosevelt. Anna had learned she was a strong smart woman of character. She'd overcome the obstacles connected with being married to a president with a disability and had impacted her world for good. She also had a good sense of politics. In fact, Anna thought she would have made a good president. That book ended up being very interesting, so Anna decided to give this book a chance. Besides, this was the only book she'd brought on this trip.

Time travel had always intrigued Anna. She had gotten hooked when she was in second grade and had started reading the *Magic Treehouse* books. She thought reading and learning about time travel was okay but experiencing it would certainly be better. Then Mrs. Mills, her fourth-grade teacher, had told the class she thought most all things were possible. Mrs. Mills believed that if you could think of something, someone could find a way to do it. Anna believed with all her heart that time travel was possible. Humans just had to find the way. People had thought about going back in time for hundreds of years, and with the discovery and study of quantum physics and quantum technology, Anna thought the time for traveling back in history was now. Her parents were engineers, and she had talked to them about traveling in time. Her dad had been less than enthusiastic, and her mom had smiled and said maybe it could happen in the future. After all, no one thought you could land on the moon until it had happened.

The author of *Friends for All Time* explained history as events in time being recorded on rays of light. These events remained stationary on the ray and could be accessed through other rays of light. In other words, historical events remained in the place they occurred. They could not be seen or accessed unless there was a change in the atoms and molecules of the human body doing the time travel. It also had to do with refracted light, accessing the correct light ray, and escaping the pull of gravity.

The author compared history to a continuous railroad track. The historical events were the wooden railroad ties, and the steel tracks were the years that connected the events. When one year ended, the next began. The friends in these books had learned that historical information was stored in a microscopic space on a light ray much like information was stored on a microscopic computer chip. They simply had to access the correct railroad tie or space on the track. In this series, the friends achieved teleportation by using laser light to create the patterns necessary for a body change to occur. The laser changed and expanded the body's molecules so it could access the historical event.

As Anna read, Robyn, Becca, Jessica, Abby, and Kelsey were getting ready for teleportation to the year 1937. Anna's eyes were moving rapidly, and she was eager to see what would happen next. One of the things she'd learned when she'd read the jacket of the book was that Amelia Earhart had disappeared while flying in her Lockheed Electra airplane. Another was the fact that she'd been the first woman to attempt to fly solo across the Atlantic Ocean from South America to Africa. Why hadn't she made it? Anna learned some people thought Amelia had landed on an island and had continued living there. Anna could imagine herself flying an airplane over the Atlantic Ocean but the disappearing part was not something she wanted to imagine. The book cover had also described Amelia as the "Queen of the Sky" and her death as being the "greatest mystery in the twentieth century."

Daniel grabbed her arm and said, "Anna, I hate it when you read. You get so into your books you ignore me. We've already taken off, and you were so involved with your book you didn't know it. Do you know where the exits are? Do you know what to do if the air pressure in the plane drops? Do you know what else? There's a man who keeps looking at you. He's already been up and down this aisle. Do I have to take care of you? I think he's trying to make eye contact with you. Don't look at him. He's the one with dark brown hair and glasses. It looks to me like that dark brown hair is a wig. He has a beard with grey hairs in it. I think he may be a predator." Then, taking a breath, he added, "No one sat in that seat. Do you think I can put my video game there until I'm ready to use it?" Reaching over Anna he laid his video game on the seat.

Anna interrupted Daniel's rambling stream of words with, "Daniel, slow down. Everything is just fine. We are just fine. Where is the man sitting?" Daniel pointed to the back of the man's head. Then Anna continued, "If he is a predator, it won't do him any good. He can't do anything to us on the airplane. If he tries we will call for help. We just need to be aware of what he's doing without him knowing we are watching him. We won't be victims. Besides, he's probably someone's grandpa who likes kids.

We'll pretend we haven't noticed him. Now, what are you reading?" Taking another breath, Anna continued, "Are you thirsty? It looks like the flight attendants are beginning to serve our snacks and drinks. What are you going to drink? Wish I liked soda. I think I'll have my old standby. Geez, listen to me, I must be nervous too. Did you really see that man looking at me? It was probably just your imagination. Guess I'll take my mind off of him by reading 'till the cart gets here. Relax, Daniel, we are okay." With those words, Anna ignored Daniel as he tried to answer her questions. She had gone back to the friends and Amelia Earhart.

Daniel, on the other hand, decided he was too excited to read and reached over Anna to get his video game. He'd played this game so often that his fingers moved automatically. He always won when he played against himself, and sometimes he beat the machine.

The rest of the trip was uneventful. Anna and Daniel ate the snack. It looked and tasted like trail mix with dried papaya and pineapple. When the drink cart arrived, Anna drank apple juice, and Daniel drank soda. There was a trip to the bathroom for Anna with Daniel standing guard, but no one bothered them. If the man was a predator, he'd given up because he remained sitting in his seat after making one more trip to the back of the plane. Ever his sister's protector, Daniel kept watch while Anna discovered Amelia Earhart had rewritten the record books with her flights.

While the kids were flying east, Ryan and his grandma had flown west and were already landing at the airport in San Antonio. Their flight had been a bumpy one, and Grandma and Ryan had played games to keep their minds off the rough flight. Ryan's favorite had been a word game using the alphabet. Grandma had tried to get him to practice the multiplication facts, but Ryan said, "No way, Grandma! I'm on vacation!" They landed, called Ryan's mom, collected their suitcases, and were waiting at the cousins' landing gate. They had been waiting for thirty minutes. Just when Grandma was getting worried, Anna and Daniel walked out the door with Zack, the same attendant who'd helped them find their seats on the airplane.

After a first minute of awkwardness between

the cousins, everyone began laughing. Grandma hugged everyone and said with relief, "Whew! You're here. I can't wait to hear about your trip. But first you must call your mom's cell, Anna, and let Daniel say hi to her too." She added, "Are we at the beginning of our journey, or are we in the middle?"

Ryan said, "Oh, Grandma, you never give up."

Grandma smiled as she said, "You can bet on that!"

Family Reunion

While Anna and Daniel talked to their mom in Long Beach, Grandma and Ryan began walking down the long concourse of the San Antonio International Airport. Catching up with the other two, Daniel said, "Grandma, I'm hungry."

Ryan chimed in with, "So am I, Daniel. Grandma said we'd eat when you got here.

Grandma, can we eat now? Maybe we could get a snack."

Anna interrupted Ryan's words with, "Daniel, don't look now, but your so-called predator is following us. He must have caught up with us when we were talking on the telephone to Mom."

Grandma looked at Daniel when she heard what Anna had said. She reacted by putting her hand protectively on Daniel's shoulder. Anna and Ryan moved closer to their Grandma, and they all turned to look at the man from the airplane. He was walking about six feet behind them. Grandma replied, "What's going on, Daniel? Who is that man? Of course we're going to look at him."

The family stopped walking, and never taking their eyes off him, they moved off to the side of the concourse. The man reacted as if he'd run into a brick wall. He quickly halted, looked around as if to find an escape, and then turned into the men's restroom. The family now stood very close together. They were all feeling uncomfortable and uneasy.

Grandma asked again, "What's going on, Daniel?"

Anna answered for Daniel by saying, "Now that's suspicious! Daniel, maybe you were right. You guys, Daniel noticed that man watching us on the airplane. I thought Daniel was just imagining it. "

Grandma interrupted Anna by saying, "Anna, let Daniel tell it. Let's just keep walking while Daniel tells us what happened. Daniel, what is she talking about?"

Daniel went through the whole story again, and Grandma replied with, "You might be right about Daniel's imagination, Anna, but we can't be too careful. Now, I want you guys to remember what he looks like. Picture him in your mind. I don't think his hair looks real. A dark brown wig might cover his real hair because you could see the edge of it around his forehead. So we don't know his natural hair color. However, remember his heavy eyebrows and big nose. He had brown eyes, but he could be wearing brown contacts. Also remember how tall he is. How tall do you think he is Ryan?"

Ryan replied, "He's about as tall as Grandpa, don't you think?"

Daniel added, "I think he looks taller because he's so skinny."

Grandma answered , "That is a good obser-
vation, Daniel. Okay, this is what we are going
to do. He knows we are aware of him because
he saw us looking at him. Now we must stay
alert and watch for him. I don't expect to see
this guy again, but if any of you do, let the rest
of us know right away. If he gets close to us,
we will call security. Don't worry, but do keep
watch."

She continued, "Now, we need to take care
of our hunger. I agree with the rest of you that
it's time to eat. I think it makes sense to eat
here at the airport because we might not get
to our hotel for a couple of hours. Anna and
Daniel, let's get your luggage, and then we can
eat before getting on the hotel shuttle for our
ride into the city. According to the map of the
airport, the shops and food are on this level.
The baggage return is downstairs. Let's find
the escalator. Boys, can you lead the way?"

The boys led the way after Grandma pointed
out the signs located on the right side of the
concourse near the ceiling. The signs were easy
to see and follow. It was not long before they
found the escalator. It turned out the food

court and the escalators were located in the same area.

As the kids started to get on the escalator, Grandma reminded Ryan to be careful how he set his suitcase on the narrow, moving stairs. Daniel quickly offered to help Ryan; the boys decided Daniel would stand on one step, the suitcase would come on the next step, and Ryan would be on the step right behind it. Both boys would hang on to the suitcase. Anna came next, and she was hanging on to Ryan. Seeing the cousins help each other made Grandma feel good. She breathed a sigh of relief as she got on the escalator with the kids. The creepy guy was nowhere in sight, and the kids were *stepping up to the plate.* They were eager to help each other.

Several planes had landed at the same time, so it took a few minutes to find the correct baggage carousel. Anna found the LA to San Antonio flight and watched as the passengers grabbed their bags off the moving beltway. They did not see the suspicious man. Anna showed Grandma which two red bags to grab, and Grandma snatched them off, checking the nametags as she set them down. The kids' mom had put bright orange tape on the handles so the bags would be easy to spot. The tape had worked.

Grandma then turned to the kids and said, "All bags are accounted for, so let's find something to eat." Daniel was the one who spotted the elevator going up to the food court and suggested it would be much easier to ride in with all the suitcases.

Ryan smiled and said, "Way to go; now we won't kill ourselves on the escalator. First one to the door gets to hold it open for the rest of us."

Food courts at airports provide a great selection of fast food, so the cousins had little trouble deciding what to eat. Anna chose Chinese food, Daniel chose a corn dog, and Ryan ate a large roast-beef sandwich. Grandma joined Ryan and got her usual junior roast-beef sandwich with lettuce and tomato. They all shared a large order of curly fries. Ryan loved curly fries. And the kids, in Anna's words, "hoovered" their food.

While the kids finished eating, Grandma

called the hotel to check on shuttle service. The next hotel shuttle would arrive in thirty minutes. They would have time to finish eating and to use the bathroom before it arrived. While they looked for the restroom, they all decided it was a good thing airports had food courts and restrooms because it was nature's way. Living things needed fuel, and living things needed a way to get rid of the leftovers. Anna laughed as she added, "We are living things, and when we gotta go, we gotta go."

Daniel replied, "Well, you could hold it. What's the longest time you ever held it, Anna?"

"It's none of your business, Daniel, but I can wait much longer than you can," she replied.

Grandma interjected, "Well I've waited as long as my body wants to, so I need a restroom now."

Anna and Grandma decided to stand guard outside the men's restroom until the boys came out. If the boys noticed a suspicious man, they were to turn and walk out quickly. Most importantly they needed to stay together. The boys would then stand guard outside the women's restroom until the women came out. Daniel punched Anna as she walked toward the restroom and said, "Anna, you're not a woman. There's nowhere for you to go. You should hold it!"

Anna replied with, "Hold it, my eye." And she punched him back.

"Okay, that's enough, kids," said Grandma as she took both of them by the arms. "There will be no fighting or hitting allowed during the next four days. Understand? "

"Okay, okay," returned Daniel, "I was only teasing, anyway."

Grandma had set another boundary for this trip, and the four travelers headed for a bathroom. Ground transportation came next, and they were standing on the sidewalk waiting when the hotel shuttle pulled to a stop. Once they were seated on the bus, they looked out the windows and decided they were traveling south on Highway 281. That road soon joined Highway 37, and in less than twenty minutes the shuttle turned right on East Commerce Street, and the family saw their hotel. It looked huge as they followed the one-way streets past the hotel, past a McDonald's, over the San Antonio

River, and turned on Market Street, stopping at their hotel. They had arrived. Anna wondered if they'd arrived at their destination. If the hotel was the destination, they had arrived. However, if the destination was the city of San Antonio, there was much more to it than this hotel. Would there be many destinations on this trip? Anna guessed she would find out.

It took little time to check in and to ride the elevator to their room. Entering the room the kids looked expectantly at Grandma as if to say, what now? Grandma answered the look by saying, "At Ryan's house it is bedtime, so goodnight everybody." Her grandkids answered her by saying, "But—we're not tired."

Anna said, "Grandma, you are teasing us again. It's early."

Grandma smiled and said, "Yes, Anna, you are right, I was teasing. I'm not tired either. I've waited a long time for this day to come, so let's start our stay at this hotel by going swimming. That should wear you kids out. Let's check to see where the pool is and when it closes. Anna, will you call the front desk for the information? The number should be there by the phone.

Boys, you can change clothes in the bathroom first, and then Anna and I will change into our suits. We can get towels at the pool." The next words out of her mouth were, "Stop! Stop!"

The boys were already opening their suitcases to look for their swimming suits but stopped and looked at their grandma to see what was wrong. She definitely had their attention. Grandma continued with, "Before we swim, we need to talk. Here are the rules for swimming. These rules are not suggestions and are not up for debate. Number one, we will wear shoes to the pool. There will be no foot diseases for us. Number two, we will wear clothes over our swimming suits because we are going through the lobby. I'll watch everything when we get to the pool. Number three is we will stay together. No swimming by yourself. I know you are all good swimmers, but we are going to err on the side of caution; safety first. Number four occurs when I say we have to get out of the pool. There will be no arguing. Number five, we will obey all pool rules, especially no running. The hotel rules do apply to all of us. Now, Anna, please call the desk to check on pool times."

By the time Anna was finished talking on the phone, both boys were ready to go. She reported the pool would be open for one more hour. They would have to hustle. And hustle they did. However, they did not run.

The water looked great! The boys took off their shirts and flip-flops, threw them at Grandma, and leapt into the pool. Anna, on the other hand, went into the water slowly, in case it was cold. Her body gave her the okay as she eased into the water, and she swam off toward the other side of the pool. The boys followed. It did not take long until they were all kicking water at each other and laughing. Grandma watched from the side and then went to get four towels and a couple of balls. She was a lazy swimmer and hated to get cold. She was more than glad to be the lifeguard for tonight.

The kids began a game of pool basketball, and it took all of five minutes before other kids joined in the game. Three older boys joined Ryan and Daniel, and the game got rougher. The boys laughed as they kicked, pushed, and shoved to get in a position to make a basket.

When Anna had enough of the roughhousing, she swam to the shallow end of the pool. A girl who looked like she was around Anna's age was sitting there watching the game. Anna said, "Hi" and asked her where she was from. It turned out Gretchen's brothers were the boys playing with Daniel and Ryan and they were also from California. Anna noticed Grandma was watching them, so she asked Gretchen if she could introduce her to her grandma. Gretchen said, "Sure." The girls then walked along the edge of the pool until they were standing next to Anna's grandma.

Introductions made, the girls decided to dive for keys Gretchen had in her bag. Each girl took turns throwing the keys while the other had to dive for it. Soon they were out of breath and had bloodshot eyes from the chlorine in the water.

At ten minutes until ten, Grandma called the kids and told them it was time for a game. They would have a contest. They would end each day by swimming in the pool, and at exactly ten minutes until ten they would have a swim-off. The swim-off required the kids to swim across the pool and then to come back two times. They could cross any way they wanted, but they had to be in the water. The first to finish was the winner. The kids' new friends asked if they could join the race and Grandma said, "Of course!" Grandma then yelled, "Go!" and the seven kids jumped into the pool. The race was on! Gretchen had raced competitively before, and she passed everyone after the first lap. Next came Ryan and Anna. Daniel and his new friend Adam came in last. The swimmers were all breathing hard and lay down on the floor by the pool to catch their breath.

At ten o'clock Grandma called, "Time to go." The kids hustled to the elevator and then up to their rooms. Good-byes were said when the other family got off first. The cousins were so tired they leaned against the walls of the elevator. It seemed like they would barely make it to their room. However, Grandma insisted a shower was still necessary because they needed to wash off the chemicals from the pool water. Grandma was the last one to shower, and the kids were already asleep when she crawled into the bed beside Anna.

Destination: Sea World

The next morning a dream caused Anna to wake up. In her dream she had been searching everywhere for a bathroom. In one bathroom all the toilets were plugged up. In another one, some big, tall girls were standing at the doors to the stalls. They were charging fifty cents to use the toilet. She had no money. She began to run, to search frantically for somewhere to go.

Was there nowhere she could use the restroom? Her bladder was screaming at her! She saw a sign saying "Restroom." She ran into the room, and it was filled with boys from school, and all of them looked at her! Her body began to feel panicky, and her eyes popped open. She sat up, looked around, and remembered where she was. She had been dreaming! The only boys here were sleeping. However, she really did need to go to the bathroom in a big way. Leaping out of bed, she made a beeline for the bathroom.

Returning to her bed, Anna started to think about the new day. She knew the schedule for the day because of Grandma's Umbrella Plan. Today they would go to Sea World, explore the two-and-one-half mile River Walk, go for a boat ride on the San Antonio River, and if there was time, they would see the IMAX Theatre's show entitled *The Alamo and the Heroes of Freedom*. The show was at the mall, and Anna's mind naturally drifted to shopping. She thought she might buy a laser light as the girls had in *Friends for All Time*. That way she would have a souvenir for two things on this trip; her book and the Rivercenter Mall. The group had decided the kids could sleep until 8:00 a.m. They would dress and eat breakfast until nine. At nine they would catch the shuttle bus to Sea World. They would be waiting by the entrance to Sea World when it opened at ten!

Anna's mind came back to the present when she heard Grandma's alarm going off. It must be eight o'clock, and that meant the boys had to get up. She would be the one to awaken them. She got out of bed, walked over to where the boys were sleeping, and then in a loud voice she said, "If you snooze, you lose! Time waits for no man." The boys slowly opened their eyes and put their hands over their ears. They immediately felt grouchy. *What was wrong with Anna?* thought Daniel as he sat up in the bed. *She's sick,* answered his brain.

Anna's loud voice awakened Grandma, and the first words out of Grandma's mouth were, "I get the bathroom first." She then headed into the bathroom carrying her clothes with her.

Daniel turned to Ryan and said, "Ryan, let's not wait to dress in the bathroom. Let's dress under the covers. Then no one can see us. Have you ever dressed under the covers? I have, lots of times."

Ryan answered, "Why would you want to do that?"

"Privacy, that's why," answered Daniel. "I can tell you don't have any girls in your family. Anna won't let me watch her dress, so she can't watch me. She has her privacy and I have mine. It was different when we were little but now she insists on her privacy, so I insist on mine."

Ryan laughed and replied, "Sometimes I wish Brady would give me privacy, and he's not even a girl. My mom says I need to let him in my room because he's so little and he wants to be with me. Sometimes it's okay, but sometimes it's not. I can understand why you want privacy. I'm game to dress under the covers if you are."

Grandma came out of the bathroom to sounds of laughter. Daniel said from under the covers, "I hate to tell you this, Ryan, but your shirt is on backwards."

Ryan returned with, "It's hard to see because it's dark under the covers. You are better at this than I am."

Anna started laughing and said, "Better watch out, I can still see you! Ooh!" She made her way into the bathroom and closed the door so she could get ready for the day. She decided she'd beat the boys ready.

Grandma heard Daniel say, "I'm better at dressing in the dark because I've had more practice. You have to do what you have to do, and Anna's the reason."

Grandma interjected by saying, "Poor Daniel, we all feel sorry for you."

Ryan crawled out from under the covers, stood, and reversed his tee shirt. He looked at his grandma and said, "Did you sleep okay, Grandma? I think I heard you snoring last night."

"Not me," replied Grandma. "I never snore."

Ryan and Daniel looked at each other, and Ryan said, "Sure, Grandma."

Smiling, Grandma retorted with, "Proper ladies never snore, and I am the most proper of all ladies."

The boys laughed, and Daniel yelled, "Anna, where are you? We beat you at getting ready."

Anna was out of breath when she replied, "You did not, and I have been ready for an hour. I've been waiting for you two to wake up." She quickly finished combing her hair and rushed out of the bathroom.

The boys looked at each other and Daniel said, "We really believe you, Anna."

A trip to the hotel restaurant came next. Breakfast would be in the form of a buffet. The kids could eat anything they wanted, but Grandma informed them she would be checking to see if they had chosen at least one thing with Vitamin C in it. She wanted their immune systems up and running. While they ate she went over the proposal for the day's activities, asking for questions and input. They looked at the official Sea World Adventure Park San Antonio Map. Grandma had written numbers one through ten on the map so the kids would have a visual guide for their visit to the park. It took about thirty minutes to finish eating and to go over the day's plans, but Grandma thought the reward would be worth it. The kids knew they would see some animal shows, would take a behind-the-scenes tour, ride a water ride, and end up at 5:00 p.m. at the Shamu Adventure Show.

The three kids were excited for different

reasons. Daniel was excited because he would get wet on the Rio Loco, a water ride. Ryan was excited because he would be able to touch a shark and see how the animals were cared for during their special behind-the-scenes tour. Anna was excited about it all. She had learned to water ski in Wyoming last summer, and she especially wanted to see the Rockin' Ski Party Show at 4:00 p.m.

The team was now dressed and ready to go. Their backpacks carried extra clothes, cameras, bottles of water, spending money, and towels. They were doused in spray sunscreen and eager to get on with the day.

They boarded the shuttle with the rest of the tourists from the hotel. The kids took turns looking at the map again as the shuttle turned south on Highway 37. A short distance later it turned west on Highway 10 and went straight through the exchange to Highway 90. The bus then went west on 90, then northwest on Highway 151. They stayed on 151 until they turned off to Sea World.

They had arrived! Grandma smiled at Ryan as she said, "Is this the destination for you, Ryan, or is it part of your journey?"

Ryan quickly replied, "I'm not sure, but this destination is just great!"

Daniel chimed in by adding, "This is a place, so it has to be a destination. It's going to be fun for all of us."

The kids sprinted toward the entrance. They knew where they were going. They had looked at the map, and they knew what the plan was. There was no hesitation. Grandma had to hustle to keep up with them. Slowing down, they passed through the entrance and then stood in single file as Grandma purchased all the necessary tickets for the day's activities.

Grandma turned to them and said, "Remember, we go first to feed the dolphins at Dolphins Cove and then to the Sharks/ the Coral Reef. Our first show, Viva, is at the White Whale Stadium at ten forty-five. Since you know our itinerary, you kids will take turns leading the way. I expect you to consult the map so you don't lead us astray. If we get lost, we'll all join in and help to find our way. Ryan, you can be our first pathfinder. Here's the map."

Ryan checked the map again and then

headed left past the bakery and treats store to Dolphin's Cove. They were just in time to feed the dolphins some food pellets. Anna reached out and touched the first dolphin while she was feeding it. It felt smooth and slick as the water ran off its face. She looked into its dark eyes, and it seemed the dolphin smiled at her! She decided its name should be Mimi. The name Mimi seemed to Anna to be a proper one for a dolphin because Mimi conjured up visions of beauty and graceful movement and smooth skin. Besides, the dolphin had smiled at her. That was enough to build a memory on. She wondered what its real name was or if the trainers even named them. She bet they did. The boys fed a dolphin too, but they had to wait in line, and they soon lost interest. Their attention spans were short because they were in a hurry to see the sharks.

The family entered the shark building just in time to hear someone talking through the speaker system. They looked around trying to find the source of the voice. Ryan spotted the diver first. She was feeding two sharks in an aquarium. As she was feeding the sharks, she was also teaching a group of people how important coral reefs were to marine life. The trainer/guide/diver went on to say the scientific characteristics of all living things were movement, respiration, sensitivity, growth, reproduction, excretion, and nutrition. If the coral reef was healthy, it provided a healthy habitat for all other marine life. That reminded Grandma that she had taught her students to remember the characteristics of living things by using the acronym Mrs. Gren. Each of the letters in the two words *Mrs. Gren* were the beginning letter of these scientific characteristics. Thus the words *Mrs. Gren* were a useful tool in memorizing them.

The group saw rays, eels, and all kinds of tropical fish besides the awesome scary sharks. A huge shark about fifteen feet long swam toward the grandkids. He swam right up to the window, and the kids thought he looked right at them. They automatically stepped back from the glass.

Daniel turned to them and said, "Hey, you guys, I have a riddle." His audience looked at him as he continued. "How do you lose weight at Sea World? The sharks eat you."

Ryan and Grandma laughed.

Anna said, "That's bad." Anna added, "Let's see if the man-eating shark will eat you!"

Daniel retorted with, "Anna, that's not a man-eating shark; the diver's a woman. Get it? I wonder why they don't call them woman-eating sharks or human-eating sharks or maybe kid-eating sharks or I know—Grandma-eating sharks."

Anna answered him, "Just humor him, Grandma. He's crazy, and he likes to hear himself talk."

Grandma answered her by turning to Daniel. "I think your jokes are creative, Daniel, and sometimes I even think they're funny. Do you remember how old you were when you started telling me jokes? You were four years old. You would call Grandpa and me on the phone, and you would say, 'You know what? I have a joke to tell you.' Then you would tell us crazy why-did-the-chicken-cross-the-road jokes. Sometimes it would be why did the hamburger cross the road or sometimes it would be a vegetable like broccoli crossing the road. Maybe someday you will be a comedian."

Daniel smiled to himself and thought, *Someday I'll show Anna. I'll be a rich and famous comedian.*

Not to be outdone, Ryan added, "I have a joke for you. What's a shark's favorite game? Don't know? Swallow the leader!" When the others barely laughed, Ryan said, "Okay, you win!"

While his cousins moved down the glass wall to see if the shark would follow them, Ryan stood mesmerized as he looked at the big creature. He thought about the marine life painted on his bedroom walls and how much better they looked in this habitat. He wished he could be on the inside with the diver. He imagined himself right there! He would swim right up to that shark and say, "Better not eat me!" If the shark opened his mouth to a take a bite, he would make a fist and bop him right on the snout. That would teach that shark a good lesson, yes, it would!

Checking the time, Grandma said, "Anna, it's your turn to lead to the Viva show. Do you need to check the map?" Anna began walking toward the exit as she checked the map. She said,

"We go right until we see the bakery and then we'll turn left. We go left past the Clydesdale Hamlet. There are three paths at the soda and snack shop. We turn right and stay right until we get to the White Whale Stadium."

They arrived at the stadium just in time for the show. Grandma suggested this might be a good time to get the cameras ready. After all, it wasn't every day you got to see a beluga whale or two. The music was awesome. It became louder and louder and more exciting until the beluga whales and the pacific white-sided dolphins and their trainers burst through the gate. They swam majestically around the huge pool. The crowd cheered and took pictures of the show. Most of all there was a cumulative desire, even a yearning, which could be felt throughout the audience that day. Everyone wished they could be down there swimming, communicating with, and touching these awesome creatures. The show only lasted twenty minutes, and that left a desire for more as the crowd hustled out of the stadium.

As they filed out of the stadium, Grandma looked at the map and said, "Let's see. Our next show is called Fools with Tools, and it is located at the Sea Lion Stadium. Will you lead the way, Daniel? Here's the map. We are here at three, and we need to go to number four."

Daniel looked at the map and then said, "We need to go back the way we came until we get to the Sodas and Snacks Store. We follow the path on the right past Shamu's Happy Harbor. At the Oaks Café and Grill, we go left past some bathrooms. Grandma, do you have to go?"

Anna interrupted with, "I don't know if she does, but I do."

Daniel continued, "At the Lorikeet Feeding area we go left past the Sea Lion Feeding Station and then on into the Sea Lion Stadium."

Everyone heard the sea lions barking when they came out of the restrooms. It turned out to be a good stop for everyone. Continuing on, the barking animals drew them quickly past the bird aviary. A crowd had gathered. The people were watching the trainers give the big, floppy, cumbersome, animals tiny fish. The noise caused the group to hurry inside the stadium.

Ryan said, "Everything seems to be eating but us. I'm hungry."

"I'm with you, Ryan. If you guys can wait, we will eat at the Sea Star Market after the show," Grandma said. She added, "We can drink some of our water and have some of the trail mix to tide us over until we can eat. We have a few minutes to wait for the show to start." Soon the kids were eating the trail mix and drinking their water.

"You may have just saved my life," said Ryan with his mouth full of nuts.

The show was crazy fun. A very funny sea lion interacted with otters and a walrus and the trainer. He also splashed water on the audience causing members of the audience to scream and run for cover. The animals' names were Clyde and Seamore. The animals got a snack every time they completed a task. This was a constant reminder of the hunger pains rumbling around in the kids' stomachs. The trail mix hadn't satisfied their hunger, and by the time the show ended, the cousins were ready to find something to eat.

It didn't take long to find the Sea Star Market. It specialized in prepared sandwiches and fresh pastries. It also had salads and fresh fruit. The kids bought peanut butter and jelly sandwiches and bananas and Grandma bought everyone a cookie for dessert. It was while they were eating that Ryan asked, "Grandma, do you remember this morning when you said proper ladies don't snore? Just what is a proper lady?"

That caused Grandma to laugh. She replied, "Ryan, that was my way of telling a joke. When I was growing up, girls were told they should grow up to be ladies. There was a whole list of things ladies should not do. Ladies were not supposed to be loud or rough. They were not supposed to spit or burp. I was told many times to sit like a lady. A lot of it had to do with using good manners, but I always wondered why boys didn't have to sit like gentlemen. Today we don't worry about being ladies and gentlemen so much, but using good manners never gets old fashioned. Now everyone is expected to use good manners. Manners do matter."

Anna added, "Our parents taught us manners, but I'm sure glad I don't have to be a lady." They all laughed at that statement.

The plan included the behind-the-scenes tour at one. They would meet the tour guide at the Interactive Programs Building. It was located in front of the White Whale Stadium. Grandma led the kids past the Haunted Lighthouse, over the Koi Feeding Bridge, past the water ski pond and the kiddie rides, turning right until they reached the correct building. The tour guide was already there.

The next hour flew by. The group became familiar with how the marine mammals lived and how they were cared for. They got up close and personal with dolphins and sea lions. They touched big stingrays, but the best part was touching a well-fed shark. These Sea World people were smart. A full shark was a happy shark and would put up with humans touching them. A mark of an excellent show, game, or tour is when the participating members are left wishing they could experience more, play more, or see more. That was exactly how each family member felt. Could someone ever get bored with interacting with nature? They decided they didn't know but they would like to find out by experiencing it all.

Daniel's Rio Loco Water Ride was next. Daniel led the way past the Water Ski Stadium to the restroom, where they put on water shoes and got towels out of their backpacks. Lockers were provided so backpacks with cameras were stored in two lockers. It was time to get wet. Grandma was not excited about this part, but she was not about to let the kids go by themselves. She did get more enthusiastic as they walked around the channel of water to scope it out. Grandma decided Anna and Daniel would ride in one of the boats, and she and Ryan would ride in the one right behind them. She thought if Anna or Daniel fell in she would leap out and get them.

Her grandkids were impatient and eager to get their turns on the ride. They had to wait about ten minutes for their turns, but they spent the time watching other kids react to getting wet. The boat riders would scream and laugh. Anna knew she would probably scream, but the boys said there was no way they would because they were men and men did not scream. Grandma assured the kids that it was okay for men to scream if they felt like it and it was likely that both of the males in the group would yell at least once. They would see.

The Rio Loco Ride was fun. No one fell out, and they all got wet. Everyone screamed or yelled, even Grandma. When the cold water sprayed them, the response was automatic. The kids wanted to go on the ride again; but the line was too long, and they wanted to eat a snack before they saw the R.L Stine's Haunted Lighthouse Show located at the 4D Sea Star Theatre .

Everyone collected their belongings from the lockers and changed wet clothing and water shoes for dry ones. However, one only had to look at the group to know they'd been playing in the water. They looked a little bedraggled. In a unanimous decision, the group decided it was time for ice cream and the flavor had to be rocky road. They bought the cones at the Rio Loco Grill and headed back around the lake to the Haunted Lighthouse Show. As they passed the Water Ski Stadium, Anna said, "Don't we go here next? Let's look at the map. I'm tired. Look how far we have to go to the lighthouse. Do we really need to see a spooky show?"

The boys chimed in, "I'm tired too." They all looked at Grandma.

Grandma replied, "What we do is up to you. Don't you remember? Two of our guidelines for this trip were the majority rules and our schedule is not set in stone. If you want to know the truth, I need a break too. How about we skip the show in the haunted lighthouse? We are already in front of the Water Ski Stadium. Let's go inside, and you guys can find a bench to lie on. We can finish eating our ice cream while we wait for the Rockin' Ski Party Show to begin."

"A unanimous decision has just been made, and I'm glad," Daniel replied. "I can't wait to sit down."

Once inside the stadium, the kids didn't lie down because the performers were warming up for the show and the music had already begun. The performers looked very young as they raced around on their personal watercraft and skied behind the cool-looking ski boat. It looked as though they were having great fun. Anna wondered if they got paid. She thought she might do this job for free. The guys were all cute, and she could totally see herself in the midst of it all.

Twenty minutes later the show began. The music got louder until a pyramid of water skiers came around an island in the lake. The girls were standing on the guys' shoulders, and the boat was going fast. The audience clapped, and some of the people yelled, "Way to go!" The performers continued to do tricks and made the tricks look easy. One guy skied on his bare feet! Anna knew none of these tricks were easy because she remembered how hard she had to work to get up on two skis. It had taken her four tries to come up out of the water and then about five more tries to stay up. Water skiing was definitely not easy, but yes, she could see herself out there. The show ended in a race with the personal watercraft. Grandma made the comment that the show was a crowd pleaser, and the kids agreed. The performers also did tricks on the speeding machines and ended up very close to the crowd. They gave autographs at the end. The cousins decided the line was too long to wait for their turn, so they exited the stadium turning right toward the next stop.

They planned to shop for souvenirs at Shamu's Emporium. They had fifteen minutes before their last show, the Shamu Adventure, started. The map stated they would see "magnificent killer whales live in an eye-popping show featuring our Shamu Visons Screen." Could they have saved the best for last? What more could anyone want than killer whales on a huge audiovisual screen? They would be the judges of this show.

As the group reached the emporium, they noticed large numbers of people entering the Shamu Stadium. They decided that if they wanted to get good seats, they probably should find them now. They wanted to be close to the water but not so close they couldn't see the screen and all of the pool. They scoped out the stadium and found some good seats. However, the stands were filling up rapidly. The family was glad they'd skipped the shopping. Anna led them to the *best seats in the house,* and they hurriedly claimed them. Now they had to wait for the show.

Grandma was a people watcher. Sometimes she just watched the audience as they watched a show to see how they reacted to it. She said the audience could be more entertaining than the show. At the present time, she was watching a group of teenagers from Japan. She figured they were from Japan because they wore hats that said Japan on the bills. They also had a guide or teacher with them. She figured the guide was responsible for the group because she was very attentive and watchful. She'd recognize that relationship anywhere because she had taken so many students on field trips. These kids from Japan were no different from kids in the U.S. They all liked to poke each other and mess around. It was not long before one of the hats was making its way through the air. The owner was close behind, complaining as he climbed over the others.

And then the music began. The sound increased to a crescendo. It was magnificent! The sights and sounds of the music and whales and their trainers made Grandma think she might be having a religious experience. The magnificence of God's world made her thankful.

Anna was amazed that Shamu was so responsive to his female trainer. The bond between the two was obvious. Was this how nature and humans were supposed to live? Was this a true symbiotic relationship? Anna decided she'd think about this later. Right now she was going to enjoy every part of this show. The highlight for her was when Shamu and his human breached clear out of the water. The trainer was riding on the whale's back! Now that was spectacular! The show lasted a short twenty minutes, and at the end, the crowd stayed in their seats. Some people were clapping, and some were just sitting there. Only one family seemed eager to exit the stadium. Then slowly everyone got up and left in an orderly manner. The crowd seemed subdued. Was this an end to a long day for people, or were they thinking about the show they had just seen? For her part, Anna was still amazed that it was possible to ride on the back of a whale even while that whale was leaping out of the water.

Standing outside of the stadium, Ryan said, "What now, Grandma?"

Grandma replied, "Do you kids still want to shop for souvenirs of Sea World? If you do, we'll go to the emporium for a few minutes before we catch the shuttle back to our hotel."

The kids agreed they should have at least

one thing to help remember this day. "What if this was the best day?" asked Daniel. It took a while for the purchases to be made. Anna bought post cards for Meghan and Allie because the girls had bought cards for her when they went on a vacation. Ryan bought a small metal shark, and Daniel bought a stuffed killer whale. He would call it Shamu. Ryan had never really been a fan of stuffed animals, so he could not understand Daniel's choice. He decided that his shark could take Shamu any time. He also decided not to say so.

The kids were pretty quiet during the shuttle ride back to the hotel. Grandma insisted they call their parents on her cell phone. With the parents satisfied, the tourists were free for the rest of the day and evening.

Destination: The San Antonio River and the River Walk

The time on the bus ride back to the hotel was spent wisely. The tired group hardly spoke to each other as they settled into the comfortable seats. Grandma relaxed so much she could have easily gone to sleep. However, she fought to keep her eyes open because she was determined to keep up with her grandkids. If they weren't sleeping, she wasn't sleeping. While riding in the bus, they finished drinking their bottled water and ate the rest of Grandma's trail mix. Both the water and the trail mix disappeared quickly. The trip back seemed to give everyone a second wind or, as Grandma commented, "I have been rejuvenated."

As they exited the bus, the family looked to the left and noticed that a long line of people had formed for the riverboat ride on the San Antonio River. They were glad that line was one they didn't have to stand in right now. They decided to go to their hotel room and freshen up.

Back in the hotel room, Daniel turned on the TV and started clicking through the channels. Anna and Ryan lay on their beds. Grandma watched the kids for a few minutes and then asked Daniel to turn off the TV. She knew it would not do to simply mute the sound because the kids would still be focused on whatever was showing on TV. She had learned this from experience. If the TV was on, these kids watched it. Parents, the telephone, grandparents, and even friends had a tough time getting their attention once the television set was on.

With the room quiet and the kids looking at her, Grandma said, "I think maybe we need to call a family meeting because we have a decision to make. As with all family meetings, everyone will have a say in the decision."

Anna's face showed her concern when she said, "Is something wrong, Grandma?"

"Oh no, Anna," replied Grandma. "I can tell you guys are tired, and I wanted to give you a chance to change our plans for the evening. We can crash and burn, which means we can eat and swim and then sleep, or we can rest for thirty minutes or so and then eat, go on the River Walk Ride, and see the IMAX movie. It's your decision to make. We can always take our boat ride and watch the movie tomorrow." The room was quiet while the kids were considering this new development.

Ryan broke the silence by saying, "Well, Grandma, I'm like my dad. I get very grouchy when I'm hungry, tired, or sick. Right now I'm two of the three, and I'm getting ready to be grouchy." The family laughed at Ryan's warning because they knew he spoke the truth.

Anna said, "I think I need to eat too. The question seems to be, do we want to eat here at the hotel or somewhere on the River Walk?"

Ryan said, "I vote for eating here in the hotel. I need food to get some energy back."

"Good idea, Ryan," replied Daniel. "We can fill our stomachs with fuel and if we decide to take a boat ride we could have dessert somewhere on the River Walk. Anyone for more ice cream?"

The cousins looked at Grandma, seeking her input. She laughed at Daniel's ice cream remark and said, "I like the idea of eating here. The River Walk is two and one-half miles long, and we're not sure where we want to eat. Let's eat here in the hotel and then decide what we want to do. If we need some down time after we eat, we will take it."

Anna smiled as she said, "I guess we decided not to decide. Can I quickly call this meeting closed so we can head downstairs to eat?" Before she could finish saying these words, all of them were headed out the door. They had forgotten to freshen up.

It was during dinner that Grandma talked

about what she liked best about the day. She wondered if the experiences of the day were different from the kids' expectations they'd discussed that morning. She reminded the kids of their individual preferences for activities offered at Sea World. Had Daniel enjoyed the water ride the best? Had Ryan had the best time of all because of his interest in marine life? Ryan thought this day had been one of his best days and had decided he would have a job at Sea World when he grew up. Anna and Daniel would not concede that Ryan had enjoyed it any more than they had. They had both had a great time and would go again tomorrow if they could. Grandma thought this was the best day she'd spent with her grandkids because she'd had them all to herself. Anna reminded her that was selfish, but Grandma insisted it was all right to be selfish once in a while.

Daniel ended this discussion when he said, "All of this talk makes me want to see what else is out there for us to see. I'm ready to go on a boat ride. Is there a chance the rest of you are feeling the same way?" The other participants to the discussion stood up together, and Daniel continued, "I guess that's our answer."

"Guess you're right, Daniel. Let's go forth. Remember to stay together. Now let's go get in that line," replied Grandma.

They waited twenty minutes for their turn to get on a boat together. They used the time to check a brochure given by the riverboat company. The brochure contained a map of the River Walk route and helpful information for someone who was new to the area. It stated they would see towering cypress trees, and stately oak and willow trees, and many beautiful flowers. There were also many restaurants. This was unique because they were located one level below the city streets. They would ride on the well-lighted river under arched bridges while the guide told them stories about the history of this interesting and amazing city. Imagine a park with shopping, entertainment, and plenty of places to eat and drink located below the city's streets! Standing near the river, the family knew there was another world going on above them because they could see and hear cars, buses, and some trucks driving over the bridges. They could also see the stairways leading up to the city streets.

Looking around, Anna said, "This is an awesome place but I could sure get lost. I'm glad I know how to read a map and that you guys are with me. This map says it's 'a traveler's best friend.' I don't know about that, but, Daniel, you'd better stay close to me. I don't want you to get lost."

"I won't get lost, Anna," replied Daniel.

Not to be left out, Ryan said, "Anna, what about me? What if I get lost?"

Anna quickly returned with, "Ryan, the same goes for you, but I know you don't get lost as often as Daniel does."

Hearing those words made Daniel complain, "See, Grandma, Anna thinks I'm still little. I haven't been lost in a long time. Anna, when you get lost, I may not show you the way! So there!"

The boats held about forty people, and the family got seats on the starboard side of the boat. If their arms had been long enough, they could've touched the brown San Antonio River water. Two young women directed the tourists to their seats and checked to make sure everyone was safe. The captain would pilot the boat, and the first mate would be their guide. The pilot's name was Jennifer, and the guide said her name was Jamie. Jamie had been a river guide for one year. She was from Wyoming and wanted to go to college where it was warm year round. She was working for one year so she could establish in-state residency in Texas. Once she established residency, her college tuition would cost less. She added that she loved this job because she got to meet so many people.

Jamie told her group the River Walk's name was Paseo Del Rio in Spanish. She said the source of the San Antonio River's headwaters was a group of natural springs that were part of an underground lake called the Edwards Aquifer. These headwaters were located very near downtown San Antonio. She said the San Antonio River was 131 miles long and ended when it joined the Guadalupe River. This tour would last thirty to forty minutes, and they would go two and one-half miles. The boats ran from 9:00 a.m. until 9:00 p.m.

The family saw crowds of people walking along the pathway by the river. Ryan was glad they were in the boat and not dodging all of those people on the shore. Crowds were hard on short people. You couldn't see where you were going, and tall people tended to push you out of the way.

As Ryan and his cousins watched, Jamie showed them the oldest tree along the walk and described the historical bridges. They'd passed under three arched bridges and were cruising to the next bridge when Ryan saw yet another bridge. That would be five bridges crossing the river in this area. Beyond these bridges was a fork in the river, and he noticed the pilot of their boat had slowed to let another boat pass. This was a busy river with so many tour boats, and Ryan decided it would not be a small task to navigate it. He thought it might be fun if the boats crashed into each other! It would be easy to swim to the side of the river because it was so narrow. He could then rescue people because he was a good swimmer. He would be a hero and would probably be on TV.

Jennifer, their pilot, turned left at the fork, and Ryan listened to their guide. She said they would be passing under another arched walking bridge and then they would see the Arneson

Theatre. Ryan remembered the name Arneson and informed the rest of the group the Arneson Theatre was where they would be performing tomorrow night. The kids looked expectantly at the upcoming structures. On the right side of the river were a small building and a large concrete stage. On the left side of the river was a small amphitheatre with concrete benches for the audience. An arched walking bridge was located on the left side of the amphitheatre. This bridge enabled people to cross the river and exit at the little white building. The building looked like a little house, and Ryan thought it was probably the staging area for props, scenery, or an area for the actors to change costumes. The river ran right through the middle of the theatre!

The story of the Arneson Theatre, according to Jamie, was that a rich man had a wife who wanted to be an actress. He wanted to please her, so he built her a stage where she could perform. Another story said the rich man had built the theatre for his girlfriend. Jamie didn't know which story was true.

Grandma announced, "Ryan, you are right.

The famous and unique Arneson Theatre is located right here. Check out the stage. Can you picture yourselves playing your instruments here? Can you picture boats going by while you are singing? Can you picture your audience watching you from across the river? "

Anna immediately said, "Wow, Grandma, you didn't tell us there would be boats between us and the audience. I can't wait to tell my parents! This is a little scary."

"Me too, this is real scary to me," added Daniel.

"I think so too," said Ryan, "I don't know if I want to do this."

Grandma replied, "We will come back tomorrow and scope out the stage. The music company will have your instruments on the stage for you. Anna, I don't know if I told you, but you will be playing on an electric keyboard. I thought that would be fine because you've played one lots of times. There will be an electric guitar for you, Daniel, and a trap set of drums for you, Ryan. There will be other kids performing, so you should have fun. I'm confident that once you play your instruments you will be glad you're performing. If it's too scary, we will just cancel. There was a waiting list of kids who wanted to perform, so I'm sure the sponsors would be able to replace you. Just remember, you are here for fun and an adventure, and this will surely be one. Not every talented kid has the opportunity to perform in a theatre like this."

Anna replied, "I don't know, Grandma. Adventure is one thing, but this is another. I don't want to be out on that stage all by myself. We need to talk about this some more."

Hearing Anna say that gave Daniel an idea. "What if all three of us were on the stage at the same time? Would that be as scary?"

Ryan interjected, "That would be better, but then we'd have to play the same song. Do we know any of the same songs? Name some of your songs, Anna. I was going to play and sing 'God Bless America.' My mom said the audience would like it because it's patriotic and they could sing along. Do you guys know that song?"

"Yes, yes we do," replied Anna. "Daniel and I both know it because we played it for a talent show at our church. Daniel played his guitar, and I played the piano. We both sang, and it sounded okay."

Daniel added, "Hey, I like that song, and I even remember it. What do you think, Grandma?"

"Listening to you guys makes me excited," replied Grandma. "I am so proud of you. I think this plan could work. I wanted this time to be fun. I didn't want you kids to be scared when you performed, so I think this would be great! You can practice tomorrow when it's your turn to take the stage. Way to go, Daniel! Now, let's listen to Jamie so we don't miss out on the rest of the river tour."

As the family had talked, the boat had continued making right turns past hotels and businesses. Now Anna checked the brochure's map and realized they were making a circle with some square corners. Jamie made the tour interesting as she described the greenery and some of the old buildings. They also saw lots of birds. Grandma reminded the kids of the time she and Grandpa had come to San Antonio during spring break and there had been thousands of birds in the trees. These birds were everywhere and were pooping on the tourists! People were walking around with newspapers on their heads to protect themselves from the bird poop. One of the birds had even pooped on Grandpa's glasses when he'd looked up! She laughed again at the memory of Grandpa trying to find something to clean his glasses with and the hordes of tourists and the poop that was everywhere. She said they still wondered what the city had done to stop the birds. Sometimes nature was not so nice.

Anna replied, "That was not healthy, Grandma. In fact, it was icky. What did Grandpa clean his glasses with? I'm sure glad the city took care of that problem before we got here."

Grandma answered her by saying, "If I remember right, neither of us had a tissue so Grandpa ended up using an old newspaper someone had dropped. It was probably dirtier than the bird poop, but at least he could see through his glasses."

Ryan was still smiling at the thought of bird poop everywhere when he noticed the boat made a left turn at a fork in the river. He recognized his hotel located just ahead. He also noticed a passing boat. The guests were all eating while the guide was talking. That would be cool to eat on the boat if the birds didn't poop on your food. He decided the people looked happy, so he dismissed the idea of birds pooping on the food.

The boat pulled into a small dock. They had come full circle and were now back in front of their hotel. Grandma tipped both the pilot and guide and told Jamie she too was from Wyoming. She wished Jamie luck and encouraged her to get back in school as quickly as possible. Grandma knew how hard it was to go to college when you were older. She had graduated from college when she was forty years old.

The grandkids were already standing on the walkway when Grandma exited the boat. The kids had decided the night was young and they needed dessert. They were not far from the Rivercenter Mall, and Grandma remembered where they could find delicious homemade ice cream. Assured they would definitely like some ice cream, Grandma led the way past another arched bridge. This bridge was located directly in front of the Rivercenter Mall and led to a tiny island in the middle of the river. People were standing on the bridge watching as the boats cruised under them. The family passed by the bridge and crossed a small stage as they entered the mall.

They spied the creamery located directly in front of them. In this family, ice cream was certainly the dessert of choice. However, their parents would not allow them to have ice cream two times in one day. It was a good thing they were on vacation. Many things were possible when they were on a trip. It had been hours since the last ice cream at Sea World. With ice cream in hand, they decided to go back outside to eat their ice cream sundaes.

A Mexican mariachi band had been on a break, and the seven men had resumed playing, singing, and dancing on the small stage. The men were dressed in special burgundy and gold costumes. The costumes looked like form-fitting military uniforms with gold braid. The music sounded complicated and would surely be hard to play. The fingers of the men seemed

DESTINATION SAN ANTONIO, TX

to fly over the strings of their instruments. They were good!

The kids were not used to this kind of music but decided the players had to be very talented to play and dance like that. Grandma reminded them they should appreciate all kinds of music. She reminded the kids that beauty in art and music was in the eye of the beholder and they were watching and listening to a traditional mariachi band. Anna wondered why there were no girls in the band but decided not to ask the question.

The kids finished eating the sundaes and threw the cups into the trashcan. Grandma could tell the sugar in the ice cream had made them hyper, and there was no way she was taking them back to the hotel to go to bed. She quickly looked at the IMAX Theatre schedule she had in her backpack. "Hey kids," she said, "there's one more showing of the movie *The Alamo and the Heroes of Freedom* tonight. Do you want to go? If you do, we will have to run to make it because the theater is located on the second floor of this mall. The show starts in ten minutes."

Daniel said, "Sure, I want to see what this Alamo thing is all about. We can make it in ten minutes easily."

Ryan said, "I don't know if I want to see it or not."

Anna added, "I vote yes because we are here now so it makes sense to see it. Besides, we'll be sitting down for the movie."

Ryan said, "Okay, let's go. The majority rules."

Destination: IMAX
Movie: a Story of Blood, Guts, and Glory

The group got their tickets and entered the theater just as the doors were closing. The previews of other movies had begun. There were several screens in this complex, and seven different movies were being shown. Grandma led the way to seats located in the middle of the theatre so the kids would feel a part of this IMAX experience. She wanted them in the center of the battle for the Alamo. She had seen this movie and knew the kids would see history through the eyes of historians. Viewing *The Alamo and the Heroes of Freedom* was not just a way to pass time; she wanted the much-researched Battle of the Alamo to come alive for the kids. Each of them had played with superhero toys. Daniel still liked Batman, and Ryan still called himself "Supy Ryan" when the occasion called for heroics. At one time or another, the Rescue Heroes—Aerial Flyer, Billy Blazes, Cliff Hanger, Jake Justice, and Wendy Waters—had become a part of their families. Now Grandma wanted her grandchildren to learn heroes were ordinary people who acted in extraordinary ways. Heroes were people who got caught up in the moment and acted courageously. She hoped her kids wouldn't be afraid when times got tough and would be willing to endure difficulties and to take risks when it was the right thing to do. She even wanted them to learn that some things were worth dying for.

She smiled and mumbled, "You are not expecting much."

As the children sat in their seats, they were witnesses to an epic struggle for land. Anna had learned in her geography and history classes this struggle for Texas was known as the Texas Independence Trail. She also knew this was new information for Ryan and Daniel. Now she learned Native American Indians had lived in the area long before Spanish soldiers and priests had arrived. History had recorded that soldiers from Spain had built five missions in order to teach the native peoples about Christianity. The Spanish had also wanted to protect immigrants coming from the Canary Islands. These immigrants had been promised the land in recognition for their service to the King of Spain.

As Anna watched this part of the movie, she wondered how Spain could control land from so far away. She knew from world geography that Spain was located in Europe, and that was a long way from Texas! Shortly, the movie addressed this question because the land was conquered again when the Republic of Mexico fought for independence and won in 1821. The land was now Mexico's to govern.

The movie continued with Anglo immigrants moving from the United States onto this land. These immigrants came because the land was cheap and plentiful. They could get a land grant for pennies per acre. They had a dream about the land and owning a place of their own. So many people took advantage of this dream the Mexican government wrote the Decree of 1830 stating no more citizens of the United States could own land in this part of the Republic of Mexico. However, the Decree of 1830 did not stop the Americans from coming, and Anna couldn't blame them. Anna thought if she could buy an acre of land for pennies, she'd do it for sure. Between the years of 1830 and 1835, the population grew from twenty thousand to thirty thousand people! The idea of illegal immigrants reminded Anna of all the people from Mexico who in the past had been illegally crossing the border of the United States to work. They also followed a dream of a better life.

Soon everyone who occupied the land

began to feel threatened. The government of the Mexican Republic felt threatened because these illegal immigrants from the United States kept coming and coming. It was not long before the Texans, as these immigrants called themselves, and the Tejanos, who were Texan-born Hispanic people, began to feel threatened by the soldiers of the Mexican army.

After that it was only a matter of time before the landowners became dissatisfied with how they were being governed, and the thought of revolution grew with the dissatisfaction. Some of the Texans and the Tejanos believed they were being singled out and were being treated unfairly. Defending the Mexican government were the Mexican soldiers who were stationed at San Antonio de Bexar, the site of present-day San Antonio.

Anna wondered when the next battle in the fight for independence would begin, and sure enough in December of 1835, a man named Ben Milam led some Texan and Tejano volunteers against the Mexican troops quartered in San Antonio de Bexar. The battle consisted of five days of house-to-house combat. Anna thought it would be shocking if soldiers came to her house in California and began killing her family! She didn't want soldiers shooting guns anywhere around her. She knew she and Daniel would be scared to death.

At the end of the five days, the Mexican General Martin Perfecto de Cos surrendered to Milam's volunteer army. Victory made the Anglos feel their cause was just and their army had prevailed for a reason. God was surely on their side. The desire to govern themselves had been vindicated. Independence from Mexico seemed necessary and proper.

Grandma watched as the kids were drawn into the plot. Their eyes never left the screen as the scenes changed. She watched them wiggle around in the stadium seats, and she heard Daniel say to Anna, "I haven't seen any blood yet." Anna shushed him and continued to watch as Davy Crockett rode into the picture with his men.

The kids had heard about Davy Crockett and his coonskin hat and had sung the song in school about him being the King of the Wild Frontier and killing bears with his bare hands.

Anna thought that was a good pun, killing bears with bare hands. Now she learned David, as Crockett preferred to be called, had brought about thirty men of the Tennessee Mounted Volunteers to join the Texas Volunteer Army. They would join in the battle for freedom from Mexico! These soldiers from Tennessee were also against the ruthless Mexican leader of the military, General Antonio de Santa Anna, and were here to support their brothers in Texas.

In war there is a saying *to the winner go the spoils.* That was another motivation for Colonel David Crockett. He was looking for a chance to earn land. General Sam Houston, the leader of the Texas military, had promised that any man who joined the Texas Volunteers would earn 648 acres of land of "your own choosing." David had described Texas as the *garden spot of the world* in a letter to his daughter dated January 9, 1836. He had wanted a chance to settle in this garden spot.

Another reason David appeared on the scene was a lost election to the Congress of the United States of America from Tennessee. He had served there before and had expected to win again. *Hmm,* thought Anna, *too bad he'd lost the election.* However, this did seem to be an example of good things coming from bad. Crockett was needed to fight at the Alamo, and if he'd won that election he would not have been at San Antonio de Bexar.

In the movie, David Crockett carried Old Betsy, his long rifle, everywhere. He said he had killed 105 bears and could shoot the wick off a candle at three hundred feet with that rifle. Grandpa was a pretty good shot with a gun, but Anna doubted he could shoot the wick off a candle at three hundred feet. Crockett was tall and strong, and some who saw him described him as a true "mountain of a man." He was famous because newspapers had described his feats and he was portrayed nightly in a theater in Washington D.C in a play called *Lion of the West.* Crocket was also famous for the buckskin vest with beaded flowers and leaves he wore, playing the fiddle, and his fine sense of humor.

The movie continued by introducing another famous hero, Jim Bowie. Anna had heard about Jim Bowie and his big sharp knife. Her grandpa had told her about Bowie when he had shown her his Bowie knife. Grandpa had used his knife for cleaning deer and elk when he'd gone hunting in Wyoming. Now, it seemed she would learn more about Bowie. It turned out he had married a Mexican woman named Ursula Veramendi. They had a family home in San Antonio de Bexar. Then his wife and her wealthy, influential parents, Governor and Señora Veramendi of Coahuila and Texas had died of cholera. This event was a tragedy for Bowie, and it was said he'd never recovered from her loss.

Bowie had considered himself a citizen of Mexico. However, like others, he had become more and more disgusted with the way the government and General Santa Anna had governed. He decided he too would support the Texas Volunteers, a unit of the Texas military. He had become known as a fearless warrior because he'd used his long knife when he fought in battles. His brother, Rezin, had given him this specially made knife as a gift. If Rezin couldn't be near to protect his brother, this knife would take care of him. And it did! It had killed many men.

Next, Bowie had been chosen to be a military leader. His reputation as a charismatic and daring leader of men had drawn the attention of the officers in the military. Commissioned a colonel, Jim Bowie was ordered to lead his soldiers against a Mexican cavalry unit at the Battle of Concepion. They'd won. After winning that battle, General Sam Houston ordered Bowie to San Antonio to "remove artillery and to evacuate the Alamo."

Arriving in San Antonio de Bexar, Bowie decided it was impossible to remove twenty cannons without horses, mules, or oxen. He also decided a battle for Texas could be fought at the Alamo and this battle would be the key to Texas independence. He began to fortify the compound.

During this time, Bowie suffered from a bout of typhoid pneumonia (some called it consumption), and he felt all of the symptoms of the debilitating disease. He coughed up blood, had the sweats, and felt weak. He'd dealt with these symptoms by drinking large amounts of alcohol. This fearless warrior was now very sick, and he was fighting more than one enemy.

Another hero of the Alamo was William Barrett Travis. He had just entered the cast when Anna looked over at Ryan. He was sound asleep with his head leaning on Grandma's arm. Anna smiled and looked at Grandma. Grandma returned the smile and put her finger to her lips as a sign not to wake him. Anna knew Ryan went to bed early at home and once he was asleep he seldom awakened before morning. She couldn't wait to tease him about sleeping through Grandma's history lesson.

The movie continued as Travis became the commander of the forces at the Alamo when Commander James C. Neill was called away for a family emergency. Travis was only twenty-six years old! He too had joined the Texas forces to protest Mexico's government. This government had been unfair to the Texans, and he had to protect the land Stephen F. Austin had given him in a land grant. He was a lawyer, and he'd just left his wife, son, daughter, and several failed jobs to join the volunteers. He had taken his slave, twenty-two-year-old Joe, with him. Anna was horrified to think that a hero would do such a thing. Then she remembered that many people had slaves during that time. That still didn't make it right in Anna's eyes, and Anna didn't think he could be a good man, but this movie was not over yet.

After joining the Texas forces, he'd led a force of armed settlers against a Mexican garrison at Anahuac on Galveston Bay. Six months later the provisional governor of Texas, Henry Smith, ordered him to the Alamo as its new commander.

Travis led approximately thirty volunteers into the Alamo compound on February 3, 1836, to take his place in history. He looked out of place as he rode into town. He seemed very young, his clothes were flashy, and he wore jewelry. A tiger's-eye ring that flashed in the sunlight was a prized possession. Perhaps it was his age or his manner of dress, but it was soon obvious to all that his leadership was not accepted and he was not respected by his troops. Colonel Bowie and his men openly challenged his leadership, as did others stationed at San Antonio de Bexar. Anna wondered how Travis could be a hero if his troops would not accept his leadership. Certainly history had portrayed Commander William Barrett Travis as a hero.

Anna learned there were other heroes at the Alamo. The Texan family of Almeron Dickenson and the Esparzas, a Tejano family who lived in San Antonio de Bexar, had joined the group inside the compound to in their words "defend the Alamo at all costs." Almeron Dickenson was a blacksmith from the town of Gonzales who brought his wife, twenty-two-year-old Susanna, and his baby daughter, fifteen-month-old Angelina, to the Alamo to keep them safe. The Dickensons were the only English-speaking, Anglo-American family within the walls of the compound.

Likewise, Señor Gregorio Esparza had decided to make a stand against the Mexican government by joining the defenders of the Alamo. In taking this stand, he also stood against his brother Francisco, who was a loyal soldado, or Mexican soldier, in the Mexican army. Gregorio also brought his wife, Señora Esparza, and daughter and four sons to the Alamo for safekeeping. The Esparza family entered the Alamo by squeezing through a small window and crawling over a cannon into the church.

Anna and Daniel got excited when Gregorio's eight-year-old son, Enrique, appeared. He was close to their age. They knew he was a hero too because everyone who had been inside the Alamo compound during this time had been described as heroic. Besides, Enrique looked a lot like Ryan. Enrique was excited to be where the action was. If there was going to be a battle, he wanted to help, especially if he could be near his father. He helped take care of his brothers and sister. He ran errands and carried messages between the adults. He also helped take care of the animals inside the fort. His father had told him to stay close to his mother and to "protect her." He'd done that, but his role as protector didn't stop him from joining in the preparations to win this battle! This was an adventure!

Since he was a child and the adults were very busy, Enrique found no one had time to pay much attention to him. He found he could go most any place in the compound. He could even leave the fort and go back to San Antonio de Bexar by way of the acequias. The acequias, or trenches, had been dug years ago to supply water to the Spanish communities along the

San Antonio River. Every child in this area had played in the acequias at one time or another. Enrique knew them well. Enrique hoped the saying *"Lo que no se ve, no se siente"* ("Out of sight, out of mind") applied to him. He didn't want to worry his parents, but this adventure couldn't be missed.

It didn't take long for Enrique to discover there were seven children at the Alamo. However, the other children stayed very close to their mothers. The men prepared for the battle while the women prepared the food and took care of the children. Enrique was proud of himself because he was helping in the fight for freedom even if the other children weren't.

The audience watched with anticipation as the background music became louder and more dramatic. The tension increased in the theater. They watched as the Mexican General Antonio Lopez de Santa Anna rode into the area surrounding the Alamo on his beautiful black horse. He looked and acted very much like a royal king. In spite of being of short stature, he was an imposing figure with his slicked-back black hair and piercing black eyes. He had been born in the year 1797 in Veracruz, Mexico, and had joined the military when he was sixteen years old. He'd become a legend when he'd fought for Spain and then had switched sides and fought for an independent Mexico. He then turned on the Mexican president and had become the president of Mexico! Later he led a coup against his own government! Santa Anna rewarded his friends and killed his enemies. That ensured loyalty and fear. He traveled with a personal staff and all the comforts of home. He ate his meals on china and crystal even during battle. He slept on linens and ate excellent food.

Santa Anna was accompanied by hundreds of *soldados* dressed in the blue, red, white, and gold uniforms of the Mexican army. His uniform was decorated with many medals and jewelry. A white plume of feathers adorned his headdress.

A second group of men arrived a short time later. Hosea Enrique Del La Pena led them. It had taken these *soldados* three months to travel the hundreds of miles from Mexico. Now the Mexican *soldados* completely surrounded the

Alamo. They were everywhere. The date was February 23, 1836.

The audience watched as the two hundred or so defenders continued to prepare for battle. They built and repaired a palisade of wood to protect the church along the south to the west wall of the compound. The palisade looked much like a log fence with very sharp points carved into the top of each log. The logs were placed vertically in the ground so anyone going over them would have to go over the sharp points. The soldiers filled the southwest corner with soil to make a platform and built a ramp up to it. That completed, they pulled an eighteen-pound cannon up the ramp to the platform. They also placed eighteen of the smaller cannons along the palisade. The troop barracks were protection because they were located along the west wall. The soldiers placed another cannon on the northwest side. The north wall was three-feet thick. Surely a three-foot wall would stand an assault. The fort seemed well fortified.

Then word came that Santa Anna had over two thousand soldiers, and the defenders knew they numbered less than two hundred men. Would more help come? They needed more soldiers! On the eighth day of the siege, a band of thirty-two mounted volunteers from the town of Gonzales arrived. They arrived expecting other troops to be there. Disappointed, the new arrivals joined with the other defenders to get ready for the attack everyone knew was coming.

Travis sent messengers to fellow citizens in other parts of Texas seeking help. He made a direct appeal to "the people of Texas and all Americans in the world" to come and help them in battle. Alas, a man named Bonham brought back the devastating news there would be no help forthcoming. These valiant soldiers were on their own!

It was then Commander William Barrett Travis became a hero. He knew he needed to inform the defenders of the Alamo of the truth of their situation. They deserved to know the truth. He called for a meeting. It was at that meeting he gave the most important speech of his young life. Admitting no help was forthcoming and the outcome of the battle could go either way, he encouraged the soldiers to defend the Alamo against the overwhelming odds. Each defender had a decision to make. Each defender could stay and fight, or he could leave the compound. As for Commander Travis, his decision had been made! Travis declared he would face victory or death!

He then gave these heroic defenders their assignments. His position would be to defend the north wall; Crockett's position was the palisade. The long barrack housed the infantry and artillery, and Bowie would defend the low barrack from his sick bed. Almeron Dickenson and Gregorio Esparza would man cannons. The women and children were to stay in the sacristy in the church. The church also housed the powder magazine. Ammunition would need to be conserved.

Meanwhile, General Antonio Lopez de Santa Anna and his troops dug in around the fort. He ordered the *soldados* to build trenches to the wall of the compound. These trenches were to be used for protection when the time came to attack. Maps were studied, strategies were planned, and the armament prepared. He flew a red flag in the steeple of the San Fernado church, and the band played the same dirge, or song, over and over every night.

The troops inside the Alamo watched Santa Anna's preparations and learned the flag was a reminder to the Mexican troops to show no mercy, to give their enemies no quarter. His orders were to kill everyone! The dirge was called the *degüello*. It was a reminder that every enemy of Santa Anna and his government must die. The *degüello* was so bothersome to the defenders David Crockett decided he'd try to combat its effects by playing along on his violin. He'd show the Mexicans their *degüello* could be made into a new song! However, the mournful, eerie music continued to make the people inside the compound restless and kept them from sleeping.

Santa Anna and his troops felt assured of victory because of their superior positions outside the Alamo compound and their overpowering numbers of soldiers. He was also willing for his *soldados* to make the ultimate sacrifice of death so he could win. He said, "Without blood or tears there is no glory." Santa Anna was so sure

of victory he proclaimed that amnesty and protection would be given to anyone wanting to
leave the compound. He then offered a three-
day truce.

When given a choice of leaving or staying to
fight the hated Santa Anna, Gregorio Esparza
said, "*Me quedo y moriré lunchando.*" ("I will
stay and die fighting.")

His loyal wife made her decision when she
said, "*Yo me quedo contigo, y con nuestros hijos
moriremos todos juntos. Pronto nos matarán. No
sufriremos dolor.*" ("I will stay by your side and
with our children, die too. They will soon kill
us. We will not linger in pain.") Hearing these
words from his parents brought the reality of
the battle to Enrique. This adventure was not
fun anymore. Could his parents really die?
Would the Mexican *soldados* really kill him?
Would his uncle Francisco kill him? Enrique
was eight years old! He was too young to die!

Hearing these words, Daniel said,
"Grandma, I don't like this. Is the whole family
going to die?"

Grandma started to answer him, but he
continued, "No, don't tell me. I don't want to
know."

Grandma watched the kids as the scenes of the movie progressed. Santa Anna's armies continued to dig more trenches closer to the walls of the compound. The soldiers and *soldados* were close enough to shout insults at each other. The insults fueled hate and the desire to kill one another. The *soldados* were here to defend their land from the hated Americans, and the defenders were here to gain their independence from the hated villain Santa Anna and his huge Mexican army. Meanwhile, Santa Anna's bands continued to play every night, and the music was torture.

Santa Anna and his forces controlled the day and night. Santa Anna's siege of the Alamo extended to thirteen days. His soldiers poured rounds of artillery on the rebels. Daniel got to see blood. Anna couldn't believe she shared a name with such an awful man. Grandma noticed that Anna hid her eyes a few times but Daniel's eyes never left the screen.

Meanwhile, the two hundred rebels returned fire with their cannons and rifles and tried to conserve the very precious ammunition while defending the walls of the compound.

On March 6, 1836, shortly after 5:00 a.m., General Antonio Lopez de Santa Anna signaled his men to attack the defenders of the Alamo compound. He sent five groups of *soldados* against the south wall fortified with the wooden palisade. They shot their escopetas, or muskets, and carried ladders to climb up and over the walls. They rushed forward yelling, "*¡Viva Santa Anna! ¡Viva Santa Anna!*" The sounds of hundreds of *soldados* screaming, "*¡Viva Santa Anna!*" and the boom and roar from escopetas and cannons were horrifying! Thuds, screams, and the cracking of wood were the sounds heard when the ammunition landed.

However, Santa Anna had designed this assault as a diversionary tactic! While the defenders rushed to counter the *soldados* on the south, Santa Anna sent his main forces to the poorly defended north wall. The construction of the wall made it three feet thick. The defenders who were left to defend it realized they had to show themselves to the enemy when they looked over the wall to fire their rifles. They could not see over the wall! Instead of offering protection, the construction of the wall had made it very difficult to defend. But defend it they did. The persistent and courageous defenders were able to kill hundreds of *soldados*. As the brave *soldados* fell, others simply climbed over their fallen comrades in the march up the walls of the compound. The ladders were placed on top of bodies, and the *soldados* continued to climb up the ladders. The battle raged, and there seemed to be blood and dying soldiers and *soldados* everywhere. The noise was loud and left a ringing in the ears. The Mexican *soldados* entered the compound at the southwest wall; they charged the ramp killing defenders as they went and captured the eighteen-pound cannon. They then turned the cannon around to fire inside the compound and killed the defenders at will.

Three groups of about sixty of the defenders went over the wall and headed for the Gonzales Road. They did not last long outside the walls. The trained Mexican troops fired on them, and no one was left standing. The Mexican army had shown "no quarter." The sound from the firing cannons and muskets slowly quieted.

The defenders had run out of ammunition and men.

Around 6:30 a.m. Santa Anna entered the compound. There were dead and dying soldiers everywhere. Only seven of the defenders remained alive, so they were prisoners of this war. One hundred ninety-three men had died defending the Alamo and had earned their places in history. Only the women, children, and slaves were saved. They had remained in the sacristy in the church for this safety. This battle had been a massacre! The rebels had been soundly defeated. The mighty Mexican army had won! Santa Anna had won.

Santa Anna was elated! He was victorious once again. He had taught the rebels a lesson. He ordered the prisoners be brought before him. History has recorded that David Crockett was one of them. Santa Anna had played the *degüello,* and his *soldados* knew they could show no mercy. No one was to be left alive! Santa Anna looked at David Crockett, and David Crockett looked back with head held high. Santa Anna raised his arm in the air and yelled, "¡*Mátenlos a todos!*" ("Kill them all!") The *soldados* aimed and fired their muskets, and the last of the defenders of the Alamo lay dead or dying. The fighting was over.

The jubilant Santa Anna retired to a small house and ordered his soldiers to bring the women and children from the sacristy to him. Senora Esparza and her children were brought before him with the others that had waited in the sacristy. Santa Anna announced, "Humane rules govern my army." He would give each remaining survivor a blanket and $2.00. He called for the lone Anglo woman and her daughter to be brought forward. Grief-stricken Susanna Dickenson had come reluctantly, and she had carried Angelina in her arms. She had prayed as she had walked through the plaza, and she had looked for her husband as she walked around the bodies. Would she be the next to die?

Santa Anna was sitting behind a desk when the Mexican *soldado* pushed her into the room. Seeing her fear, Santa Anna said, "I do not make war upon women and children. Neither do I make war on slaves. Humane rules govern my army." He then tried to give Susanna money and a blanket and offered to send Angelina to Mexico City. There he would pay for her education.

Susanna refused his offer, and Santa Anna replied with, "Then go tell the Mexican rebels what happened to those who dared to oppose me. Describe it exactly. Say it will happen to them. You will also carry a letter to all Texans willing to obey Mexican law once again. Colonel Almonte's orderly, Ben, will go with you to make sure you do as I command. All of you Texans are fools because it is impossible to fight me and win. Tell them Santa Anna is coming."

The frightened and grieving Susanna and Angelina Dickenson left in a hurry with the letter. Ben accompanied them. The letter from Santa Anna said,

Citizens! It became necessary to check and chastise a parcel of audacious adventurers, Bexarians! Return to your homes and dedicate yourselves to you domestic duties. Inhabitants of Texas! The good among you will have nothing to fear.

Signed Antonio Lopez de Santa Anna

Soon the Dickensons and Ben were met on the road by scouts from General Sam Houston, and Susanna told her story.

If Susanna and Ben had looked back, they would have seen black clouds of smoke coming from the war-torn Alamo. As a last sign of domination and to further humiliate the rebels, Santa Anna had ordered the bodies of the defenders to be burned in a funeral pyre. Only the Mexican-born defenders were to be buried. Santa Anna had taken his revenge!

The movie ended with General Houston's scouts saying, "We will remember the Alamo! Remember the Alamo!"

Winners, Losers, and the Good Guys

The family relaxed as the credits were super-imposed over flashback scenes from the movie. They had been witnesses to a massacre! They had struggled with the Texans. Grandma turned to them and said, "It's very late, so we'd better wake Ryan and get started to our hotel."

"Okay, Grandma," replied Anna, "I think

we have some things to talk about after seeing this movie."

Daniel interrupted her with, "That battle was not fair. There was no way two hundred defenders could win against thousands of soldiers with plenty of guns and ammunition."

"So, Daniel, would you say the defenders of the Alamo were fighting against impossible odds?" asked Grandma. "Was there ever a time in the movie you thought or hoped they could win?"

"I thought the good guys were defending the Alamo to gain freedom for the Texans and the Tejanos, and of course I hoped they would win. It seems like if you are doing the right thing you should win. I didn't know they were all going to die," answered Daniel.

"Do you guys know who ended up winning the land in the end?" returned Grandma.

"Obviously the Texans and the Tejanos won since the land is now part of the United States. As someone said, they lost the battle but won the war," stated Anna.

By now Grandma had Ryan on his feet, and they were headed out the door. Ryan, still trying to wake up, said, "Did I miss anything important?"

That question caused the other three to laugh, and Grandma said, "Did he, kids?"

"Ryan, you missed blood and guts and glory! You missed death, destruction, sacrifice, suffering, and honor!" answered Anna.

"And you missed loud cannons going off! They were so loud I thought I might have to plug my ears," added Daniel.

"You slept through all of that, but it's all right; you will find out what you missed when we tour the Alamo compound," replied Grandma.

Ryan answered with, "Well, I didn't miss it all, but it sounds like I missed the best part. Were there really lots of blood and guts?"

"Oh, yeah," answered Daniel, "and the Mexican army stomped them in the ground. They whipped them, and then they humiliated our soldiers when they piled up their dead bodies and burned them up! That's called a funeral pyre, by the way, when you pile up bodies and burn them. "

"Okay, okay, let's head back to the hotel, and

we'll talk on the way," interjected Grandma. "It's very late, so we need to be careful while we walk. Watch for anyone who seems to be overly interested in us. If you see anyone suspicious let the rest of us know."

As they walked out the door of the mall and headed down the River Walk toward their hotel, Grandma asked, "Anna, you said we needed to talk about the movie. What part did you want to talk about?"

"Well, Grandma, I just don't understand war," she answered. "Why did so many people have to die? Why did they hate each other so much? Why did so few people have to fight against so many? And what would have happened if the defenders had refused to fight?"

"Why, then they would be cowards, Anna," replied Daniel. They had to fight to prove they should own the land. That's what I think, anyway."

"Okay, Daniel, what is a coward? Is it better to be a coward or dead?" asked his sister.

"I think a coward is someone who is afraid to fight for what he believes in," answered Daniel.

"Could we also say a coward is someone who knows the right thing to do but is afraid to do it?" asked Grandma.

"I think I don't want to be a coward any-time," interjected Ryan. "I don't want anyone to think I'm too chicken to protect and fight for my family and what's right."

"All I'm saying is, could there be a better way to solve problems?" answered Anna. "Do people have to kill each other to prove they are right?"

No one said anything more until they were ready to enter the hotel. Grandma said, "Anna, I don't know all the answers, but it seems to me you should be right. People shouldn't have to kill one another. We should be smart enough to settle our differences without violence. However, history records there have always been wars with people killing each other, and we know that history seems to keep repeat-ing itself. Historically, men and countries have fought over the right to control and own land because that gives them power and money and resources."

"What about the people who fight for their

religion?" asked Daniel. "They want everyone to believe in God the same way they do. How is that different from fighting over land?"

"Good question, Daniel. I hadn't thought about that reason to fight a war just now, but there have been many wars fought in the name of religion," answered Grandma. "I wonder if wars have been and always will be fought because humans don't know any other way to settle their differences. Many very smart people have tried to solve the problem of war for thousands of years, and we still have wars. So I guess we probably won't solve it tonight. We can talk some more about it tomorrow when we're not so tired."

Anna interjected, "Now that we are almost to our room, do we have to shower, or can we just go to bed? After all, we did get wet on our boat ride."

"Don't remind me," answered Grandma with a sigh. "That was hours and many germs ago. Guess you guys can wait until morning, but I'm showering tonight. However, there's no way I'm letting you sleep in your clothes, so, boys, you use the bathroom first, and after Anna I will use it. Then Grandma left the kids to fend for themselves while she called Grandpa to say goodnight. Calling Grandpa was a nightly ritual when they traveled without one another. By the time she showered and came out of the bathroom, the grandkids were sound asleep.

The Rock Stars Perform

The next morning Grandma awakened to whispering voices. She sat up in bed and looked around for the source of the whispering. No kids were in sight, but the sounds were coming from behind a partially closed bathroom door. She crept out of bed and moved closer to the voices.

She heard Daniel say, "It's one thing to play

for family and church, but it's another thing to play for strangers. What if they laugh at us? What if we make a mistake? I just don't know if I want to do this."

"We don't want to hurt Grandma's feelings, but I tend to agree with you, Daniel," replied Anna. "It would be different if Dad and Mom were here. What if the audience boos us?"

Ryan laughed and said, "Anna, who will know if they do boo us? The people in the audience will never see us again anyway. They don't know us, and we don't know them. I think it would be easier to sing and play for strangers than for people who know you. I get scared to death to perform in front of my parents."

"Guess you're right, Ryan. I didn't think about that part. Since this is a family weekend on the River Walk, the audience will probably be made up of the families of the performers. They wouldn't be as likely to boo as teenagers would. You never know what teenagers will do. They know what they like, and if they don't like your music they will let you know," continued Anna.

"We won't ever see the audience again

unless we get rich and famous from singing on the River Walk," added Daniel with a laugh. "It's not like it's a competition or anything. We would be singing for the fun of it and for Grandma."

"Anna, what if we practice to see if we sound terrible? If we do sound bad, we will cancel like Grandma said. I sound pretty good by myself, if I have to say so; and you and Daniel have sung together, and you know you sounded okay. Besides if you guys mess up, I will play my drums really loudly until no one will be able to hear your mistakes," said Ryan, with a grin. He continued with, "Nothing ventured, nothing gained."

"Ryan, what if your drum playing is gross? I've never even heard you play. Maybe I will sing and play loudly enough to cover up your mistakes," teased Anna.

"No, you are both wrong. I will play the electric guitar so loudly I will stop people in their tracks! I will be the star, and you will play backup for me!" yelled Daniel.

Grandma decided now was the time to join the fun. She did not want the kids to know she had been listening to their conversation, so she said, "What's going on? Why are you yelling, Daniel? The neighbors will think something is wrong and will call security."

At this point Daniel was so excited he couldn't help himself. He continued in his loud voice, "Grandma, we've just decided that I am going to be the star of our group tonight! Our group will be called Daniel and the Backups! Yes, and everyone will cheer me because I am the star! I am about to become a rich and famous rock star!"

By now Ryan and Anna were yelling too. Anna yelled, "You will be the star over my dead body! Our band will be called Anna and the Boys! I will be the rich and famous one!"

Ryan laughed and yelled, "No! No! You have it all wrong! Drums rule! Our band will be called King Ryan and the Serfs! Yes, King Ryan and the Serfs has a nice sound to it. I will be the star, and you will carry my drums for me!" And with those words he laughed as he ran over to the bed and fell on it.

"What visions you have for yourselves," answered Grandma. "I have the best vision!

The band will be called Hot Grandma and her Rock and Roll Band. While you guys sing and play, I will dance!"

The vision of Grandma dancing on a stage really cracked the kids up. Grandma dancing in front of people could never happen. It was a matter of honor for the family. She couldn't even get Grandpa to dance with her. Poor Grandma!

"Okay, I guess it's time to come back to the real world now, kids," Grandma said when the kids quit laughing. "Have you decided whether you are going to perform tonight?"

Anna looked at the boys and said, "Have we?"

"I think Ryan's idea about seeing how we sound after we practice this afternoon is a good one. I'm scared, but he's right when he says nothing ventured, nothing gained. Grandma, will you be honest and tell us if we sound terrible? You don't have to worry about hurting our feelings," answered Daniel.

"Of course I would be honest, but I've heard all of you sing, and you are good singers. Why would you start sounding terrible now? What about you, Ryan, how do you feel about performing?" asked Grandma.

"Well, if I have to share the spotlight with someone else I guess it might as well be my cousins. Maybe my fame and fortune will rub off on them," Ryan answered with a smile.

Anna interjected with, "Yes, Ryan, we know how famous you are. Daniel and I will help you get started in the business."

Grandma added, "I guess that's a yes to performing this afternoon. I think our chance to practice is set for one o'clock. You guys are scheduled for a thirty-minute practice so you can become familiar with the instruments. We need to make two copies of "God Bless America" so Anna and Daniel will have the music. We can do that while we are at the mall. Tonight's show time is scheduled for seven o'clock, but you will know if you're playing after you practice."

"What are we going to do until then?" asked Ryan. "I don't remember our "Umbrella Plan" for Saturday."

"I think we talked about touring the Alamo today, Ryan, but I don't think we will have time to do the Alamo justice. As I was lying in bed, I thought we might go shopping at the Rivercenter Mall this morning, eat lunch wherever we choose, and then go to your practice. Behind the amphitheatre at the Arneson Theatre is a shopping center called LaVillita. There are lots of artists with shops there. Do you remember the multicolored windmill I put in the raised flowerbed in the backyard? Grandpa and I bought it at one of the shops when we were here last time. I want to go back there and buy a souvenir of this trip," answered Grandma.

"That would be a good gift for my dad's garden," added Anna.

"It would be good to get our parents' gifts today, and then we don't have to worry later," suggested Daniel. "Do you remember when we talked about El Mercado, the largest Mexican market outside of Mexico being in San Antonio? Maybe we could go there to shop. Maybe we could find some cool souvenirs. They should have authentic Mexican souvenirs."

"That's a good idea, honey," replied Grandma. There is a streetcar on Commerce Street that will take us to the El Mercado or

Market Square. It's inexpensive and fun to ride on. The hours are very user friendly, so we could get back in plenty of time to get ready for your performance tonight. I have a map of the downtown streetcar routes so we can see where to get on the streetcar."

Ryan interrupted the plans. "Is anyone hungry besides me? I'm starving!"

"Way to go, Ryan, thanks for looking out for my stomach," replied Daniel. "As Great-grandpa Stevens sings, 'Let's eat, I'm hungry. I'm in the mood for food. You're sweet and lovely, but I'm in the mood for food.'"

"He used to sing that song to me when I was a little girl," said Grandma. "I didn't know he'd sung it to you guys too."

"Too bad he's not here to play the harmonica. He could play in our band tonight. He's a good musician," added Anna.

"Let's eat breakfast here in the hotel so we can get started on our day," suggested Grandma. "Last person ready has to clean up the hotel room. We shouldn't leave a mess for housekeeping."

The family scurried around to get ready.

Daniel and Ryan were dressed and ready first, then Anna, and then Grandma. While Anna was finishing with her hair, Grandma began picking up the clothes that had been left on the floor the night before. The kids turned the TV on while they waited for their Grandma to get ready. They knew Grandma would not leave the room until she had her makeup and her hair done. She said she wanted to look her best no matter whom she was with. She said when she looked good she felt good about herself.

The family took a bathroom break before leaving the hotel. Breakfast had been devoured quickly, and Grandma insisted she didn't want anyone in their group worrying about finding a bathroom. Then they headed to the mall with Grandma holding their music.

Anna looked at the quiet beauty surrounding them and said, "It must take a lot of people to take care of this underground park. I wonder when they work. I haven't seen anyone who looked as if they were working down here. I will never forget this trip, and now that we are going shopping I want to find just the right souvenir for sure. I think I want to buy something that will last a long time. It should be something small so I can keep it forever. I've been thinking I might want to find a laser pen for my souvenir of San Antonio."

"Why would you want that, Anna?" asked Ryan.

"If I bought a laser pen I could kill two birds with one stone," answered Anna. "I'm reading a book, *Friends for All Time.* It's about girls traveling back in time. To transition and transform themselves, they make patterns with the pens. If I buy one it will be for two reasons. One reason is to remind me of the book and number two is I will have a souvenir from the mall in San Antonio. See, I will kill two birds with one stone. Get it? A laser pen would also last a long time, maybe forever."

"Yes, yes we get it, but that sounds like three reasons to me," replied Daniel. "Maybe you will kill two birds with three stones or three birds with three stones. You need to get your birds and stones right. At least you know what you want. I wish I knew what I wanted. I also wish I could go back in time. That would be great."

Grandma interrupted Daniel's ramblings

with, "Kids, I've been trying to figure out the most efficient way to shop. I think maybe we ought to stay together. It's not that I don't trust you guys to behave, but I don't trust other people. There are too many weird things going on in the world today. So, since Anna knows what she might want to buy, we will all look for a shop that sells laser pens. Then we will go where you boys want to go. I think we should go to the information booth to find a store that sells the pens first."

As they came closer to the mall, the family noticed there weren't many people on the River Walk. The mall opened at ten o'clock. They would have ten minutes until the doors opened.

Anna was still enjoying the beautiful underground park when she said, "Stop, can you guys smell those flowers and hear the river? It's hard to notice things like that in a crowd of people. Early morning might be the best time to enjoy the River Walk," said Anna.

"I feel like jumping into the river. It would be fun to float along," replied Ryan.

"It would be fun until a cruise boat came

along and ran over you, Ryan," laughed Daniel. "Besides, look how brown the river is. I think there's pollution in it."

"I think the cruise boats should rent tubes and let tourists float the river sometimes," interjected Ryan. "They could ban boats or any vehicles with motors for say two hours in the early morning to ensure safety for the tubers! It would be great fun to paddle along in the water. The pollution would probably settle during the night, and there would be no boats to stir it up until after ten o'clock. Sometimes I amaze myself with my good ideas."

They arrived at the front doors to the mall about five minutes before they opened. As they sat on the stairs and waited, Grandma said, "Kids, think about what we learned from the IMAX movie. Think about all the historical events that have happened in this very place. Remember Enrique, the Tejano boy who was eight years old? I'll bet he played somewhere near where we are sitting. This would have been a good place for one of those ditches the Spanish people built to get water from the San Antonio River. Do you remember they were called acequias? Can you imagine how fun it would be to play in the water in an acequia? It would be an excellent place to play hide and seek in if it wasn't too full of water. I wish the ground could speak about the things or events that happened on or around it."

Anna answered her grandma with, "Well, I think the ground does talk. Doesn't an archeologist dig in the earth for fossils and artifacts? The artifacts then tell the history of an area. That's kind of like the ground talking."

"I guess you are right, Anna, artifacts are records of the people who lived here," answered Grandma.

"I think I might be an archeologist when I grow up. That sounds like a great job," said Daniel.

Anna was laughing when she replied to Daniel, "Daniel, it would take four lifetimes for you to have all the jobs you'd like to have. It's a good thing you have many years before you have to decide on one or two jobs."

Daniel replied, "Remember Dad's friend Adam? He's had about ten jobs. So, Anna, there is hope for me."

"Well, I think history keeps marching on, and we can sit here and let it pass us by, or we can go shopping," Ryan interjected. "The doors to the mall have been unlocked. Let's be about making some history of our own."

The tourists soon found the information desk, and the lady who worked there was very helpful. She said there was an office supply store on the second floor and showed them where it was on a map. As planned, they would go there first. As they turned a corner, the kids heard the sounds that could only come from an arcade. Guns were shooting, whistles were blowing, paddles were smacking, and there was a constant dinging of bells to signal the players of points being scored or games ending. "Please, Grandma, can we go in there after Anna gets her pen?" asked Daniel. "I'll pay for my games with my own money. I've spent hardly any money, and it's burning a hole in my pocket."

"Do the rest of you want to play?" asked Grandma. "I can't believe the arcade is busy already."

"Yes, yes," replied Ryan.

"Me too," added Anna.

"Then it's settled," said Grandma. "We'll go there as soon as Anna is finished. Since the store is an office-supply store, they will probably have a copy center, and I will get the copies of your music made. I think I will get one extra copy made in case something happens to one of them."

Once inside the store, Grandma left the three kids at the laser-pen aisle while she went to make the copies of the music. When she returned each kid was holding a laser pen.

"What's going on?" she asked. "I know why Anna wanted one, but what about you boys?"

Ryan answered, "Grandma, it's like this. I didn't even know I wanted one until we found these pens. They are awesome. They are electromagnetic and have a cycle of 532 nanometers, whatever that means. This says it projects to more than five miles, and it only costs $20.00. I can't pass up a bargain like that. It is also a flashlight! For that price I can find something to do with it. My dad will be proud of me for getting a bargain!"

"Same here," interrupted Daniel. "And we won't get the pens mixed up because we each got a different color. Anna got teal green; I got my favorite color, royal blue, and Ryan chose a light blue one.

"Well I'm glad you got what you wanted and got a bargain," said Grandma with a laugh. "I do wonder what you will do with a pen that shoots a laser for five miles, though."

"Daniel just can't stand for me to have something he doesn't. That's all. Now Ryan has one too, wouldn't you know? They are copycats; that's what they are," Anna retorted.

"Now, Anna, be nice," replied Grandma. "When someone copies you, it's a compliment because they think your idea is great."

"Well at least I won't have to share if they have their own," replied Anna. "Let's go pay."

Once in the arcade, the kids hurried around the room to check out the games and machines. Daniel found one with airplanes shooting down airplanes. Ryan's game had to do with shooting baskets with a basketball, and Anna's had racing motorcycles. Grandma insisted the kids should buy the tokens to play the game while she was there to monitor how much they spent. Their enthusiasm for these games could become very expensive quickly. They played until Grandma said they needed to get going if they were going to do any more shopping for Anna. It had been a fast thirty minutes! The boys had used up all their tokens, but Anna had one left. She quickly put it in her pocket. It would be another souvenir.

Anna soon found a clothing store for teenage girls. The boys refused to go inside, so Grandma followed Anna and periodically walked back to the front of the store to check on the boys. Anna bought a sleeveless red shirt with a striped scarf. The scarf could be used for a belt or could be worn around her neck. Anna had other shirts she could wear the scarf with, so she was pleased with her purchase.

When Anna and Grandma joined the boys, Grandma said, "I have a good idea. What do you think about wearing the same color of shirts for your performance tonight? Anna just bought a new red shirt. What if we find a tee shirt shop, and I will buy you boys new red shirts? Then you'd really look like a group."

"Well, Grandma," answered Daniel, "real rock bands don't wear the same clothes at all. What if Ryan and I got different colored shirts?"

"I agree with Daniel," said his cousin.

"Okay, let's do it," agreed Grandma.

It did not take long to find another tee shirt shop, and the new shirts were quickly purchased. The family found themselves walking around the mall wondering where to go next. The boys only wanted to look in sporting goods stores, and Anna was happiest in the clothing stores. They were saved from themselves when they noticed the time on a clock above a store.

Anna said, "If we are going to eat before we practice, we need to do it now."

Daniel replied, "I'm too nervous to eat. Let's eat after our practice."

"Once again, I agree with Daniel," said Ryan. "I can't eat if I'm nervous. I guess boys just think alike and stick together."

"I do think it would be good to be at the Arneson Theatre early so we can listen to other performers. Then we can compare your music and song to theirs," suggested Grandma.

It took little time for the group to reach the Arneson Theatre. The family listened while a girl around Ryan's age belted out a song about love and being jilted. They decided she had a good voice but did not like her song. The next act was two brothers who were really good dancers. They incorporated stepping and hip-hop dancing.

The cousins were next, and Grandma walked across the bridge with them to the stage. They checked out their instruments and carried them onto the stage. Grandma helped Ryan to set up his drums and seat. Then she helped Anna connect her keyboard to the electric cord and then arranged the stool behind the keyboard. Lastly, she helped Daniel. He decided to stand to play, but he did need help getting connected to his electricity. Grandma got music stands so they could see the music and signed for the microphones. The kids were set!

A young man walked over to them and said, "Wait a minute. I thought the next performance was a solo. I think you guys are practicing out of order."

"We are sorry if we have caused a problem, but the kids decided they wanted to perform as a group instead of doing solo performances. I know I signed them up as soloists, but could we please change our plans?" asked Grandma.

"Our program is really long tonight, so a group performance is really preferable. I think that will work out fine," he replied. "My name is Mike, and I will be the announcer. I will make the changes on the master sheet so there will be no confusion. Does your group have a name? I will need your information: your names, ages, and the name of the city you are from. While you kids are practicing, maybe your grandma will fill out the paperwork." Then he told them they would be the third act on the program and a crew would be there to make a video of their performance. Grandma could buy DVDs when she gave their information to the woman in the corner. He ended the instructions with the words, "Your thirty minutes are about over, so if you are going to practice, you'd better hurry."

The practice went better than Grandma expected. The kids warmed up on the instruments and had time to go over the song two times. The next performer was waiting when they finished, so there was no time to worry about how they sounded. They all hustled to get their instruments off the stage and into the little white house for safe keeping until time for the performance.

Grandma was smiling when they finished and walked over the bridge to the amphitheatre. Before the kids could ask the all-important question, Grandma said, "You guys sounded awesome! Your voices blended well. Anna, you could be a little louder, but I am so excited! I wish your parents could be here to listen to you tonight. I paid for the DVDs so they will be able to enjoy your performance later, but I wish they could be here to see you in all your glory! Before we go, you have one more thing you need to do. You need to decide if you want a name for your group and, if you do, what it is so I can tell the information lady."

The kids gave each other high fives, and Anna said, "I think we need a name that sounds like a family since that's what we are. What about The Cousins?"

"What about Two Boys and a Girl?" interjected Daniel.

"We are not just two boys and a girl,"

returned Ryan. "I like The Cousins better I guess. Let's go eat. I'm hungry now."

"Then The Cousins it is," replied Grandma. "Please stay here while I tell her."

The rest of the afternoon went as planned. They ate at one of the shops at the La Villita shopping center, and Grandma got her windmill. She chose a windmill that looked like a multicolored merry-go-round. The kids weren't too eager to look at the jewelry or pottery the artisans had made, so they had found their way to the streetcar and had ended up at the El Mercado. They spent about an hour there looking at piñatas, sombreros, and pottery. They ate a cookie in the bakery. They liked the apothecary shop with all the strange medicines the Mexican people used the best. They saw snakes in big jars and all kinds of plants, spiders, and insects. They were supposed to cure all kinds of diseases. The kids decided it was better not to know what was in their medicine. The idea of eating spiders, insects, and snakes was not appealing to them. Grandma was glad the kids were grossed out and enjoyed their discomfort.

They arrived back at the hotel with plenty of

time to eat a snack, shower, relax, watch a little television, and dress in jeans and their new tee shirts. Ever the drama queen, Anna repeated, "I'm scared, I'm scared," about a thousand times until Daniel told her to be quiet because she was freaking him out. For once Grandma was happy the kids got so absorbed with television because the time went by quickly. The kids had called their parents and then had left for the Arneson Theatre by six o'clock.

The talent show started promptly at seven p.m., and The Cousins were ready to get their performance over with. Grandma kept reminding them to live in the moment, to try to enjoy this moment in time, and to make a good memory.

Anna said to her Grandma, "You can be all philosophical because you are not the one performing!"

Soon the kids were on the stage with Grandma standing in the wings watching with great pride. She wasn't performing, but she was nervous. She wanted this performance to go well for her grandkids. This performance was part of the journey, and no one could ever take this experience away from them. They had performed on the great Arneson Theatre stage!

And then the music began. The kids sang, "God bless America, land that I love. Stand beside her and guide her through the night with the light from above." To Grandma's ears this was music from heaven! She heard each instrument and each voice, and her heart soared with the joy of it. And then she noticed the audience sitting across the river in the amphitheatre had started clapping and singing with the kids. After all, this was a song they knew. Most everyone knew all the words! Then some of people in the crowd stood up. They continued singing and clapping as The Cousins repeated the song twice. And then it was over. The Cousins bowed and then began taking their instruments off the stage. The audience continued standing and clapping. The applause was not just in appreciation for the performance but was an expression of their pride and love of their country. This performance had been an opportunity to show their patriotism, and they were not afraid or embarrassed to show it.

Soon the family was hugging, and tears ran

down Grandma's face as she thanked the kids for their performance and said this had been one of the best times in her whole life.

Destination: The 1836 Battle of the Alamo

The performers and their grandma found seats in the amphitheatre and sat down to watch the rest of the show. There was a brother-sister singing act, a comedian about ten years old who wasn't very funny, and some kids who sang solos. Next, there were a couple of good drummers and some more dancers. It was hard for The

Cousins to sit quietly after their performance because they had been so pumped! The kids wanted to be polite, but they found it very difficult to sit still. They tapped their feet, clapped their hands, and shifted their bodies around. Finally Grandma whispered, "Come on, kids, let's go celebrate your stardom. This show is between acts, and I don't know how many acts are left. I think we have been polite enough. What would you like to do to celebrate?"

As they walked down the River Walk, Ryan replied, "Well I'm—"

Before he could complete his sentence, his cousins chimed in with, "hungry!"

They all laughed, and Grandma said, "I guess we've learned even rock stars have basic needs. Everyone gets hungry. The basic needs do not change when you become famous."

"Grandma, you know we didn't get famous tonight," replied Anna.

Grandma continued, "Yes, I know, but you are famous in my eyes. Besides, we didn't see anyone else get a standing ovation. I thought The Cousins were the best! However, I'm sure each family thought its kids were the best.

That's what families are for. Now what do you guys want to eat?"

Quietly Daniel said, "I think some ice cream might help settle my stomach. I haven't had any ice cream for days."

The other kids laughed at his comment because they had been thinking the same thing. What could be better than ice cream at a time like this?

Grandma said, "Well, kids, I wish this family could celebrate without food, but we don't seem to know how. We are already on a trip, so we can't celebrate with a trip. It's too late to go to Six Flags and ride the rides. I guess we could go shopping and spend money, but we don't know what we want to buy. I guess we could say, I scream, you scream, we all scream for ice cream!"

"Yes, way to go, Grandma! We all scream for some ice cream!" yelled Ryan.

"Okay, this is what we'll do," answered Grandma. "We'll go back to our hotel room, use the bathroom, call your parents to let them know how well you did, and then we'll get any kind of ice cream you want. Tonight you can even have banana splits if that sounds good to you. You don't have to eat all of it. We can watch what we eat tomorrow. Besides banana splits have fruit in them."

"Good plan, and I think I'll take my laser pen with us, because we might need a flashlight before the night is over," replied Anna.

"If Anna takes hers, I'm taking mine," added Daniel.

"Me too, if they have theirs, I will take mine," said Ryan.

"I don't plan to get off the lighted path tonight, but you guys can take them if you want. Just don't lose them," returned Grandma, "and please be careful where you shine the lasers."

It was not long before the family was sitting at a table in front of the Rivercenter Mall. They were each eating a banana split. Sharing was not even considered. Tour boats passed by on the river, and they watched as the boats went under the arched bridge located in front of them. They looked at the tiny island located in the middle of the river. There wasn't much conversation as the family indulged in the most sumptuous feast of all. The kids had never eaten a whole banana split. Grandma reminded them to be sure to eat the bananas, strawberries, and pineapple and to eat just until they were full. They were not to stuff themselves. She wished she didn't feel guilty about feeding the grandchildren so much ice cream.

Daniel and Ryan finished eating every last bite. Grandma and Anna were horrified. The boys were stuffed. They felt so good! They were enjoying the results of all the sugar. They felt hyper!

"Hey, we haven't crossed the bridge to the island yet," Daniel yelled. "Ryan, let's go exploring!"

"If you're going, so am I," replied Anna. "The colors of the flowers are spectacular. I see purples and reds and blues. Look at those orange flowers. What kind are they, Grandma?"

"I don't know about the orange ones, but from here it looks as though there are some purple pansies and some red carnations. You guys need to run around a little and work off your sugar," answered Grandma. "Why don't you go over to the island and check it out? I'll wait here because I'm tired and a little sleepy."

Grandma watched as the cousins raced across the bridge to the island. Ryan won the race. She watched as they walked carefully around the island trying to avoid stepping on the beautiful flowers and the spotlights. She watched as her grandchildren used their flashlights to further inspect the flowers, and she noticed the lights were soon changed to laser points. She thought the lights were pretty, but she wondered what effect lasers would have on the flowers.

Meanwhile, the grandkids were in a huddle around the bush with orange roses. They were shining their lasers on it when Anna said, "Daniel, do you remember when you said you would like to go back in time?"

"Sure, Anna, but I'll probably never get to," answered Daniel.

"What about going back now? We could do like the girls did in *Friends for All Time,*" suggested his sister.

"Tell me again what they did," demanded Ryan. "I can't remember what you said before."

"Well, in the book, the girls use quantum physics and laser technology to travel back into history. I don't understand all there is to know about quantum physics, but it has to do with the smallest amount of radiant energy and sub-atomic particles. In the book it's about changing energy—that's us—from one form into another. It's also mind over matter. You not only use laser beams; but you also must believe it can happen for your molecules in your body to change, and that involves your brain. In the book time is stored microscopically in the area or space where it happened. In other words, when an event like the battle at the Alamo happens, that event remains stored on waves like light waves in the space or area where it happened. Remember how we talked about the ground talking to archeologists? Well, the atmosphere around the earth has also recorded historical events. When conditions are right you can access that time and space."

"Wow, Anna, how do you know all that?" asked Ryan.

"I hate to say it, but Anna knows about lots of things. She reads all the time," interjected Daniel.

"I think I want to travel in time like the

girls in my book," said Anna. "Anyone want to go with me?"

"Whoa!" said Ryan. "How and where would you go?"

"I'm thinking I'd like to go back in time to just before the final battle of the Alamo. Wouldn't it be cool to meet Enrique?" returned Anna.

"But, Anna, remember all of the people at the Alamo died. Why would you want to see that?" asked Daniel.

"The women and children didn't die. Santa Anna released them. I don't think we would have to worry about dying," answered his sister.

"I guess if you're going, I'm going. Someone has to take care of you," added Daniel.

"But how are you going?" asked Ryan. "Is this really possible?"

"I believe it is possible with all of my brain," replied Anna. "It's just a matter of time until lots of people time travel. I even think someday people will take their vacations back in time. Wouldn't it be cool to watch Alexander Graham Bell invent the telephone? I'll bet he would freak out if he could see all our cell phones and what we can do with them now."

"You have a big imagination, Anna, but if you guys are going, so am I," said Ryan. "You can count me in. Do we need to invite grandma to come? My parents will be really mad if we don't come back. Now what do we have to do to get to the Alamo?"

"Grandma said she was tired. Let's let her rest until we see how all this works. Are you guys ready? To begin teleportation we need to make patterns with our lasers. The girls in the book stood in a circle and started at their feet. They started by pointing their lasers to their right and spiraling the light around and around the circle. The lasers began to change the molecules in their solid bodies. The patterns made by the lasers caused them to disappear from the present back into time. They do the same thing to come back to the present only they move the lasers in a pattern going left," Anna continued.

"Wow, I hope you know what you are doing, Anna. I just think you do. Let's go for it!" exclaimed Daniel.

The kids stood in a tight circle so none of

the laser beams could escape. Anna began the change by counting to three. The laser lights came on, and their marvelous adventure began. By the time the lasers reached their heads, the grandkids were gone.

The kids were still standing in the tight circle when they realized they had been transported back in time. They were standing in a ditch with about two to three inches of water in it. They quickly clicked off their lights and put them in their pockets. They didn't want anyone to see them until they were ready to be seen.

"I think we did it!" squealed Anna.

"Shh! God help us!" said Daniel.

"He will, you know," answered Anna. "He never leaves us, no matter what."

Ryan interrupted with, "You guys, we need to be smart about this. Do you hear those cannons and the long rifles firing? They are firing real bullets, and they could hit one of us! I don't know if it's the right thing to have done, but we did this, and now we have to make the best of it. He continued, "I'm not dying out on this battlefield! We need to find our way into the

Alamo. We'll be safer there. We need a plan. Do you see the Alamo over there? It looks like this ditch goes toward that church. I think we should stay in it and get as close to the Alamo as possible before we crawl out of this ditch. What do you guys think?" Then he added, "I don't think there were any blond-haired children our age at the Alamo, so we need for the blond-haired kids in this group to add some camouflage."

Anna replied, "Ryan, everything is okay. We will be smart. Just remember, we know how this battle ends. We will keep down so none of the Mexican soldiers see us. Heaven forbid, they might shoot first and ask questions later. I agree that Daniel and I need to disguise our hair. I can use my scarf to tie my hair down and cover my head. I have seen many Mexican women with their heads covered with scarves. Daniel, I think you should rub dirt in your hair to change its color."

"Shh! Someone is coming," whispered Daniel as he rubbed dirt in his hair. The cousins lay down in the canal and remained as still as possible. Daniel could feel his heart beating, and it was hard to breathe. Water soaked into his clothing, and he thought he felt some kind of insect or spider crawling on his shoulder. He'd be okay as long as it wasn't a snake. What if it was a snake! He didn't dare move a muscle, or they would be found out! Keeping quiet was a matter of life and death! Looking up the ditch he could hear and see someone coming toward them crawling on his hands and knees. He heard terrible, eerie-sounding music coming from everywhere. Bright lights were flashing in the sky from the shells that were exploding over them. Daniel almost said, "Are we having fun yet?" but he thought now was not the time for humor and stopped. In the past when he was scared he could tell a joke, and laughing would help his fear. Now he felt fear from deep inside him, a fear that kept him from saying a word, a fear that threatened to shut down his brain. From somewhere inside him the words "Daniel, you can do this" flashed in his mind. He took some deep breaths, his brain settled down, and he was ready. Ready for what he didn't know, but at least he was ready.

It was then he heard some men talking in

Spanish. They were not far from them! He understood some of the words, but they were talking so fast he could make sense of only a few of the words. They had to be the *soldados,* and they seemed to be talking about Santa Anna and his orders for his army. They were talking about the possibility of dying in the battle tomorrow.

Anna was lying in the ditch in front of the boys. The person in the ditch continued crawling toward them in the dark. She said, "*¿Quién eres? ¿Nos ayudas llegar al Alamo?*" ("Who are you? Will you help us get to the Alamo?")

The kids sat up in the canal when they could see the person was a boy. Could it be Enrique?

"*Me llamo Enrique. ¿Cómo se llaman ustedes?*" said the boy. ("My name is Enrique. What are your names?") Then he smiled.

Anna smiled back and answered, "*Qué gusto verte. Nos ayudas, ¿sí?*" ("We are so glad to see you. You will help us, yes?") "*Queremos ir al Alamo. Puedes llevarnos alli?*" ("We want to go to the Alamo. Can you take us there?")

Suddenly the kids heard the *soldados* coming toward them. The men peered over the edge of the ditch, and one of them said, "*¡Mira! Hay cuatro niños en la acequia. ¿Los matamos? Pueda que estén espiando por los rebeles.*" ("Look! There are four children in the acequia. Shall we shoot them? They may be spying for the rebels.") The *soldados* pulled up their guns and were aiming them at the kids when they heard Enrique say, "*Tío Francisco, no dispare. Soy yo, su sobrino Enrique Esparza.*" ("Uncle Francisco, don't shoot. It's me, your nephew Enrique Esparza.")

His Uncle Francisco replied, "*Enrique, qué hacen ustedes en esta acequia? No saben que es peligroso estar acá afuera? Estamos en plena batalla. Vuélvanse al Alamo donde pertenecen. Váyanse ahora! No quiero verlos acá fuera otra vez. Váyanse o los mato yo mismo¡ Tu padre es un traidor!*" ("Enrique what are you kids doing here in this acequia? Don't you know it's dangerous to be out here? There's a battle going on. Go back to the Alamo where you belong. Go now! I don't want to see you out here again. Go now or I will shoot you myself. Your father is a traitor!")

Enrique had no choice but to turn around

and head back toward the Alamo. The visitors followed closely behind. They were so quiet they were scarcely breathing. They had never been this close to death before! So far this adventure was not fun. It was downright scary! Enrique's Uncle Francisco watched the kids with his gun drawn until he could no longer see them and then returned to his group of *soldados*.

As soon as the kids thought the uncle could no longer see them, they stopped. They took a big breath and with it breathed a sigh of relief before they started talking.

Enrique said, *"Ustedes hablan como gringos. ¿Son gringos? ¿De dónde vienen?"* ("You speak like the Anglos do. Are you Anglo? Where do you come from?)"

Anna answered, *"Sí, somos gringos. Hemos venido a visitar desde otro tiempo."* ("Yes we are. We have come to visit from another time.")

"Cómo se llaman? No entiendo de dónde son, pero están bienvenidos a entrar al Alamo. Es peligroso acá fuera." asked Enrique. ("What are your names? I don't understand where you are from, but you are welcome to come into the Alamo. It's dangerous out here.")

Daniel interrupted with, "*Me llamo Daniel, mi hermana es Ana, y mi primo es Ryan.*" ("My name is Daniel, my sister's name is Anna, and my cousin's name is Ryan.") "*¡Gracias, gracias por salvarnos las vidas!*" ("Thank you, thank you for saving our lives!")

Ryan added his thanks by saying "*¡Gracias, gracias! No hablo español muy bien; lo siento. Mucho gusto en conocerte. Eres un héroe. Sabes héroe?*" ("Thank you, thank you! I don't speak Spanish very well; I'm sorry. I am glad to know you. You are a hero. Do you know hero?")

Enrique replied, "*Sí, sé lo que es héroe. No soy héroe. Mi padre es héroe. El dispara un cañón. El no es un cobarde como dijo mi tío.*" ("Yes, I know hero. I am not a hero. My father is a hero. He shoots a cannon. He is not a traitor like my uncle said.")

"*Creemos que eres un héroe, porque nos salvaste de los soldados, Enrique,*" returned Anna. "*Nos llevas a donde están los niños y las mujeres en el Alamo? Pienso que estaremos salvos allí.*" ("We think you are a hero because you saved us from the soldados, Enrique. Will you take us to where the women and children are staying in the Alamo? I think we would be safe there.")

"*Sí, sí*," answered Enrique. "*Estarán salvos allí. Síganme.*" ("Yes, yes. You will be safe there. Come follow me.")

The next few minutes seemed surreal to the visitors. At the end of the ditch, Enrique led them into the Alamo by crawling through a window into the church. They were dripping wet and muddy from the water in the acequia. The kids didn't have to worry about camouflage because they were covered in dirt and mud and looked almost as dark skinned as Enrique. They looked around and marveled at their surroundings. The cracking sounds from the constant bombardment of the shells from the Mexican army combined with the morbid music were enough to terrorize the bravest kid. They had seen the IMAX movie, but it didn't begin to touch the fear in the voices and eyes of the people inside the compound. These defenders of the Alamo knew they were outmanned and outmaneuvered, and their supplies of ammunition were running low. They had seen the red flag flying from the church and knew Santa Anna would show no mercy. He meant to kill them all. They were all going to die. They didn't know when they would die, but they knew it was a matter of time until they would. They had chosen to stay and fight for their freedom from Mexico, and they would pay the ultimate price of death.

Enrique first took his new friends to his mother, who was still cleaning up from cooking the evening meal. The women had used up most of the food because this siege had lasted thirteen days. The men had needed to eat to retain their strength, and the children always seemed hungry. The women had stretched the food by adding water to the soup and cutting the size of the portions. There was not much food left, and Enrique's mother knew they could not last much longer. She had no idea how they would feed three more children.

Señora Esparza introduced the visitors to Susanna Dickenson. Señora Esparza thought she might as well put Anna to work babysitting Susanna's baby, fifteen-month-old Angelina. That would free up Susanna to help with the work the women were expected to do. Besides Anna looked like a strong healthy girl, and they needed all the help they could get.

Anna was thrilled to take care of baby

Angelina even though the baby was fussy. Anna had taken a babysitting class, and she felt sure she could quiet a fussy baby. Sure enough the baby stopped crying as soon as Anna held her in her arms and whirled around the room with her. Anna soon had her cooing and laughing. Angelina said, "Water." Anna got her a drink, and when Anna put her down on the floor Angelina could walk pretty well. Angelina tripped and fell sometimes, but Anna kept close watch on this darling child.

Enrique took Daniel and Ryan with him to check on his dad. When the boys found him, Señor Esparza was still manning his assigned cannon. He looked exhausted but was glad to see Enrique. He said he was concerned about David Crockett. David had not played his fiddle for several hours, and Señor Esparza was worried he'd been wounded. Would the boys please go check on him? Enrique hugged his father before he left. This was a scary time, and he needed his dad's reassurance.

The boys found David Crockett defending the palisade wall. He was sitting with his back to the wall with his head in his hands.

Enrique stood by while Daniel and Ryan talked to him in English. Speaking Spanish was hard for the boys, so they were glad when they could speak their own language. Mr. Crockett seemed pleased when the boys asked if there was anything they could do to help him. David Crockett suggested they might want to go check on Jim Bowie. He said Jim was very sick and could probably use a drink of water. It was then David Crockett stood up! Daniel and Ryan were amazed at how big he looked. The words "mountain of a man" came to Daniel. Bravely Daniel said, "Mr. Crockett, I understand you play the fiddle. I play a guitar. They are a lot alike. If I had my guitar here we could play a duet. Please sir, could I touch your violin? I promise I won't hurt it."

And just like that, David smiled and put his arm around Daniel. He said, "Why sure, son. Do you want to play it?"

Daniel answered, "No, sir, I just want to be able to say I touched your fiddle and heard you play. Yes, and I want you to know I think you are a true hero."

Then Mr. David Crockett said, "Well, I'd

thought I was too tired to play my fiddle anymore, but you boys have given me some new energy. That blasted *degüello* is driving me crazy. I think I'll just go up on the wall and try to drown it out. I think I will turn the *degüello* into a song to dance to. That will show Santa Anna. See you later, boys. The next song will be played just for you. Stay safe."

In the meantime, Anna was getting to know Angelina Dickenson better. She was an armload to carry around. She was heavy. The room in sacristy was small, and Susanna had told Anna she was not allowed to leave it with Angelina. Anna's arms were hurting from carrying Angelina, so she sat Angelina on the floor in the corner with her. No shells from the guns could reach them there.

She pulled the token she'd saved from the arcade out of her pants pocket, and she and Angelina began to play a hide-and-seek guessing game with it. Anna would hide the token somewhere in her clothes, and Angelina would find it. When she found it, she would laugh and hold it in her hand. When she started to put the token in her mouth as all babies would,

Anna took it away from her and hid it again. Angelina was smiling and giggling. Anna was glad she had a toy to keep her occupied. They'd been playing hide and seek with the token for a few minutes when Anna heard a man's voice. She knew the token had to be hidden because it would cause questions Anna was not prepared to answer. She looked for somewhere to hide it and noticed a geode located about two inches from the floor where they sat. She quickly put the token in the hole in the center of the geode. It fit perfectly!

A man entered the sacristy with Susanna Dickenson. Susanna introduced Anna to the commander of the Alamo, William Barret Travis. He had come to see Angelina. Susanna took Angelina from Anna so Travis could talk to the baby. The commander was holding a gold cat's-eye ring on a string. Gently he put it around Angelina's tiny neck. While he was putting it around her neck, he explained the ring was very special to him and he figured it would be safe with Susanna and Angelina. He expected to die in this battle, and he thought the Mexican *soldados* would spare a baby and would not take his ring.

The boys came into the room just as Travis was finishing his explanation. Mr. Travis took one last look at the ring and then walked out of the small room. The boys quickly told Susanna they had been sent by David Crockett to fetch water for Mr. Jim Bowie. As Susanna went to get the water, Anna whispered to the boys, "It's getting late, and if we plan to make it out of here before the final assault on the compound, we'd better go now. Otherwise the Mexican army will be using the acequia as cover for their assault. There will be no chance for us to make it out alive if they catch us in the acequai."

When Susanna returned with a flask of water, Anna asked Susanna if she might go with the boys to give Mr. Jim Bowie his water. Anna said she was good with sick people and maybe she could make him feel more comfortable. Susanna agreed that maybe Jim Bowie needed Anna more than she did. The cousins left with Ryan carrying the water in the flask.

The kids knew Jim Bowie was lying in a small room on this south side of the compound. That made him close by. They stayed close to walls for protection and watched for problems like flying bullets as they carefully made their way to his room. They heard Mr. David Crockett serenading them from the wall. He was playing the song "Turkey in the Straw." He was as good as his word!

Before the kids entered the room, Ryan called out, "Mr. Bowie, Mr. Crockett asked us to bring you some water! Would you like a drink?" The kids entered the room and saw the dying man lying in bed with pistols in both hands. They did not want to startle him. It would be awful to be shot by friendly fire.

Jim Bowie opened his eyes and in a weak voice said, "Thank you, son, I am very thirsty. A drink of water would make me feel better, so I can kill me some *soldados*."

Ryan came into the room with the water and soon realized there was no way Jim Bowie could sit up to drink. He asked Anna to help him hold up Mr. Bowie's head so he could drink the water. Gently Ryan and Anna supported Mr. Bowie as he took several swallows of water before closing his eyes and lying back down.

The kids smelled a putrid smell in the room and looked around trying to find the source.

They soon realized the smell was coming from Mr. Bowie and his bed. Anna bent over to smooth his blanket so he could be more comfortable. When she moved his blanket she saw the biggest knife she had ever seen lying next to his leg. She showed the knife to the boys and both of them moved closer. The knife was huge, and the boys couldn't resist touching it. Anna's turn was next, and before she could touch it, Jim Bowie said, "Don't touch my knife. I have killed many men with that knife and plan to kill some more when the Mexicans come. I once cut a man's heart out with it."

After hearing those words, all three kids turned and ran out of the room without saying good-bye. They were out of breath by the time they arrived back in the sacristy. Anna immediately turned to the boys and said, "We will talk about this later. We have to leave the compound now. We can't wait any longer, or we won't get out. If we say good-bye to anyone it will only cause questions. Follow me."

Daniel and Ryan did not argue as they followed Anna out of the window and dropped into the acequia. They quietly crept along through the water as if their lives depended on it. They heard bugles blowing and Mexican *soldados* marching closer. It would not be long now before the final battle would be fought. The kids could feel the excitement and tension in the air. It was almost like feeling electricity. It made their skin tingle, and if their hair could have stood on end, it would have! History was being made, and the cousins knew how this battle and the war would end. This experience was awesome, but the kids couldn't wait to get away from it! They had experienced enough history!

They finally arrived at the end of the acequia. This was the exact spot they had started from. The cousins stood together in a tight circle and pulled out their laser pens. Anna reminded the boys to shine the lasers to their left and the pattern began. By the time the pattern reached their heads the kids had emerged from the past to the present! They were back!

The Arcade Token and Destination: Six Flags Fiesta Texas

The time travelers turned off their laser pens and remained in their tight circle. The kids checked each other to make sure they had made it back in one piece. They were so excited at the successful conclusion to their trip they started jumping up and down. "We're back! We're back!" they yelled. It was Anna who came to her senses first. She said, "Stop jumping up and down, you guys; people are looking at us. They will think something is wrong with us."

"Touch me. Am I real?" asked Ryan.

"Touch me too," added Daniel. "I feel way different."

"We are different," answered Anna without touching either boy. "After what we just experienced, we will never be the same again. Do you know anyone who has traveled back in time? I don't. We will just have to deal with the changes. Let's find Grandma. I hope she's not worried about us."

Ryan asked, "Are we going to tell her what we did? This would be a hard secret to keep to ourselves."

"Let's play it by ear. Let's see what Grandma says, and we will go from there," answered Anna.

The kids started walking over the bridge, and by the time they reached the River Walk, Grandma was standing there waiting for them. She said, "Kids, what's up? The oddest thing just happened to me while you were on the island. I was daydreaming while watching you use your laser pens on the orange flowers, and the next thing I knew, I couldn't see you anymore. I know the island is too small for three big kids to hide on. You weren't hiding were you? I guess I must have dozed off. A fine Grandma I am, I must be more tired than I thought."

The kids looked at each other as Grandma continued, "When I saw you jumping up and down just now, I thought, oh my word, the kids are still full of sugar from the ice cream. We have one hour until the swimming pool closes so if we hurry you guys could swim and burn off some of your excess energy. Let's go for it, okay?"

The family walked quickly back to the hotel. Everyone was out of breath as they entered the hotel room. While Grandma was in the bathroom, the grandchildren decided their adventure had been too great to keep to themselves. They just had to tell someone, and Grandma needed to know so she could join in their excitement. When she came back into the room, Anna said, "Grandma we need to tell you something. Please don't get mad when we tell you."

Grandma's voice registered her concern when she said, "What has happened? Are one of you sick? Why should I be mad? I thought we were having a good time."

Daniel's voice couldn't contain his excitement as he said, "Grandma, do we have a story to tell you! Are you up for a life-changing story? Anna, you'd better start first, but I want to tell my part." With those words the boys sat down with Anna on one bed, and Grandma sat on the other.

Anna continued, "I don't know quite how to tell you, but, Grandma, we went to the Alamo without you."

"You did what? Why? If you wanted to go to the Alamo tonight, all you had to do was tell me, and we all could have gone. I don't know when you had time to go. Besides I think the Alamo is closed to the public at night," replied Grandma. "Now I'm confused and concerned, but I'm certainly not mad."

"Grandma, please listen to what we have to say, and then you will understand," interjected

Daniel. "We didn't mean to do anything wrong, and as it turned out, our trip was awesome."

"Daniel, I'm supposed to start the story, so please let me," continued Anna. And for the next thirty minutes or so, the kids told their story of the Alamo. It was a story with a destination and a mind-bending journey. Anna told Grandma about time travel and how they used quantum physics and their laser pens to get back in time, about Enrique, and about babysitting fifteen-month-old Angelina Dickenson, and how Angelina got Colonel Travis' cat's-eye ring for a necklace.

Daniel told about Enrique and how they had talked to him in Spanish and how Enrique's great adventure had turned into a horrible nightmare. He went into detail about how Enrique had saved them from getting shot by Enrique's uncle Francisco Esparza and the other Mexican *soldados* because they had thought the kids were spies. When he said those words, Daniel looked at his Grandma, and she looked horrified! That Grandma was horrified was good. He smiled and continued with his story of David Crockett and how Mr. Crockett had let Daniel touch his fiddle and about the mournful, eerie-sounding *degüello*. He told how Crockett had changed the song by playing "Turkey in the Straw" and how his playing the violin seemed to make the defenders of the Alamo feel better. He ended with, "And Grandma, in real life, David Crockett was a bigger hero than the IMAX movie showed because he was kind to a kid, and that kid was me!"

Not to be outdone, Ryan chimed in with his story about the dying Jim Bowie, who had lain in his smelly bed with his eyes closed. They had known Mr. Bowie had been ready to do his part in the final battle because he had been holding two pistols, one in each hand! Ryan said, "Now that is a brave man!" Ryan told about Bowie's thirst and about giving him the glass of water.

However, the best part of the story was about the huge knife with the sharp blade that Jim Bowie had in bed with him! Ryan said, "There lay Mr. Bowie barely breathing with his trusty weapon! At the end of his life all he needed was his knife!" He could hardly contain his enthusiasm and excitement when he described how he and Daniel had bravely touched the knife that had killed so many real people! His eyes were huge as he told how the kids had run when Mr. Bowie scared them with his words about cutting men's hearts out.

Lastly, Ryan told how scared he was that he might die when shells were exploding around them as they were hurrying to leave the Alamo. He told Grandma about the relief he felt when the cousins had stood in their small circle and turned their laser pens to the left. And then he said with a smile, "Too bad Anna didn't get to touch the knife! Boys rule."

Grandma felt many emotions as she listened to their story. She was excited; at times she was frightened, and most of the time she couldn't believe her ears. She had many questions, but she could not doubt the veracity of the kids' story. They believed what they were saying. Could the kids have gone to sleep and dreamed about the Alamo? That didn't make sense. Could eating so much ice cream have caused such a sugar high the kids had hallucinated? That thought was ridiculous. She finally decided she would choose to believe it really happened because her grandchildren believed.

She did not want to ruin their awesome experience with questions the kids probably couldn't answer. The thought crossed her mind that she might be a little afraid of some of the answers and where they might lead. She chose to sleep on this information, and maybe she would have some answers in the morning. At least she hadn't gone to sleep while she was watching the kids. She hadn't been a bad grandma after all.

She asked the kids if they wanted to call their parents and tell them about their adventure into the unknown. Each kid decided he or she wanted to wait until they were home and the story could be told face to face. Their parents would be more likely to believe them and not be scared out of their minds if the kids were sitting in front of them when they told their story.

Grandma replied she had a plan for the rest of the night. It was too late to go swimming, so tonight would be a good movie night. She did not expect them to be ready for sleep so they all would take showers, and after they were ready for bed, they would rent a movie and watch it until they were sleepy. Tomorrow morning they would go back to the Alamo, and the grand-kids could show their grandma exactly where they had been.

Watching the movie put them all to sleep. Grandma woke up when the movie went off. She turned off the TV and the rest of the lights and checked the kids. They were sleeping quietly and peacefully. Grandma smiled as she thought that time travel seemed to agree with them.

The grandkids awakened Grandma the next morning. They had dressed quietly so she could get some extra sleep. However, hunger pains and the desire to hurry to the Alamo compound cut their good intentions short. Grandma awoke to see and hear three kids standing over her yelling, "Time waits for no grandma! Food and the Alamo wait for us!"

It was a good thing Grandma was a morning person because she smiled as she rolled out of bed and said, "Okay, okay, you kids watch TV while I hurry to get ready. I'm impressed that you all are ready to go this early. I'll hurry as fast as I can."

The time travelers wolfishly ate their breakfasts and headed down the River Walk toward the mall. They would go back to the bridge where their adventure started, see the acequia, and then cross through the mall coming out on the other side facing the Alamo Plaza. They would cross the street and walk into the church.

The kids relived the trip through the acequia, where they first met Enrique and almost got shot. They remembered the wet clothes and being afraid. Anna remembered they had crawled from the acequia to the wall of the Alamo and then had crawled inside the Alamo through a window. The family looked for the window but was unsure which one it could be. Things did not look the same as they had last night. They decided the window would be easier to find from the sacristy where the women and children had stayed for safety.

It was in that small room that Anna remembered playing in the corner with Angelina. She explained why she had decided to sit there with the baby, and she reenacted that part by walking over and sitting down. She could almost feel Angelina's warm body and how tired her arms had felt from carrying her. Anna continued her story about how she and Angelina were playing hide and seek with the token she had left over from the arcade. She explained why she had hidden the token in a geode in the wall. Anna said, "Then I heard a man's voice talking to Susanna, and in walked Colonel Travis, the commander of the Alamo. He was carrying a gold cat's-eye ring on a string. I looked down like this to make sure the token couldn't be seen, and there it was. And—*there it is!*" As Anna was saying these words, she reached into the geode and picked up the token! Holding it out for the others to see, Anna started yelling, "It's here! Here it is! You guys can see it, right? This proves we were here last night! It *was* real!"

Hearing the noise, a guide hurried into the room, and in a hushed voice she said, "If you can't be quiet, I must ask you to leave. This is a sacred place, and we insist everyone treat it as such. You will be quiet!"

Grandma returned, "We are very sorry we were talking loudly, and I can assure you it will not happen again. My granddaughter just got excited about all the history that went on in this room. We will be quiet."

The guide gave them a dirty look, turned on her heel, and walked out of the room.

The kids and grandma circled around Anna, and Grandma whispered, "Well I'll be. It certainly looks like your token, Anna."

Daniel said, "This is too much for my brain to handle. I'm freaked out!"

"I can't believe it, either," added Ryan.

"Shh," reminded Grandma. "You kids will get us kicked out of the Alamo. Let's go outside, and then we won't have to be so quiet."

Once outside, Daniel said, "Please can I hold the token, Anna?

Grandma said, "We all want to look at and touch it. I know Anna will share." The kids and Grandma took turns holding the token. They were holding a piece of history, and that history belonged to Anna! The bronze-colored token wasn't worth much to others, but to Anna and the boys it was worth millions of dollars. This was a one-of-a-kind souvenir that Anna would keep forever! This souvenir had also done something for Grandma. The bronze-colored token had made Grandma a believer! She didn't understand how this had happened, but she believed it had been real.

Everything that happened at the Alamo after that was anticlimactic. The family quietly returned to the sacristy and looked at the objects displayed in a well-guarded case. They saw Colonel William Barret Travis' gold cat's-eye ring, David Crockett's beaded buckskin vest, a long rifle, a powder horn and gun, and a knife once owned by Alamo defender Jacob Durst. Lastly and best of all, they saw Jim Bowie's huge knife! To think the boys had touched it! It did not seem as big as they'd remembered, but it was still huge as knives go.

They retraced their steps of the night before, but it was not the same. They thought they found the room where Jim Bowie had been, but that looked different. They tried to picture David Crockett standing on the wall playing his fiddle, but even that didn't feel right. Sensing the kids' discontent, Grandma reminded them the Alamo had been only partly restored to its 1836 condition, and it had gone through many changes before the restoration. She suggested they might want to leave the partly restored Alamo compound now and come back tomorrow when the kids might feel differently. Besides, the sky looked like it might rain, and the Umbrella Plan had included a trip to Six Flags Fiesta Texas for the afternoon. Leaving now would ensure an earlier start.

The kids agreed with Grandma, and the tourists headed back to the hotel to get ready for Six Flags. They planned to have lunch at the theme park and see at least one of the shows. This vacation was awesome; if one destination didn't satisfy, they could simply go to another.

They finished planning for the afternoon in their hotel room. Grandma got out her information for the theme park, and the kids took turns reading it. They had learned from experience the time spent planning would pay positive dividends. Since they were going to eat lunch at the park, Daniel read the dining options. They were numbered with red circles and marked on the map provided by Six Flags Fiesta Texas. The kids decided they wanted to eat at number seven, the Old West Barbeque, because they thought it would be fun to eat a big turkey leg.

They could also have corn on the cob. Daniel thought he might eat steak on a stick.

Since this theme park had won the award for Best Theme-park Shows in the Country, they decided they needed to take in at least one show. Ryan read the descriptions given about the shows, and after considering the time and information about them, it was decided they should attend "Batman Forever" located at number one. They circled the number on the map.

Anna read the information about the rides. The rides that were recommended by the theme park for families were marked with a yellow *F.* Grandma suggested that since it would probably rain they should ride on rides that would not be closed because of the weather. The kids also decided to ride on the rides marked with the *F* to ensure safety. They would ride on number one, Batwing. That was described as a chance to feel the sensation of flying above Gotham City. That should be fun after just seeing the show "Batman Forever." They marked number one on the map. From there they would go to number sixteen, Shipwreck Falls. That was described as an exciting water-bound excursion that sent riders plunging over a fifty-foot waterfall into a tidal-wave splash! After they survived that ride, they would go to number six, Disaster Canyon. At Disaster Canyon they would experience the thrill and adventure of white-water rafting as they whirled through churning, surging rapids. They could hardly wait.

From there, they would go to number twenty-six, the Island Kingdom Water Park, and while there, they would ride number twenty-nine, the Castaway Creek Ride, and number thirty, the Commotion Ocean wave pool. The Castaway Creek was an action river with geysers, water bubbles, and waterfalls. The kids already knew what a wave pool was. They would remain at the wave pool until they were tired and wanted to go back to the hotel. They could check the bus schedule at any guest-relations booth to see when the buses left. These booths were marked on the map with a yellow smiley face.

The family decided to wear their swimsuits under their shorts and shirts. Since Grandma would be riding the rides with Ryan, they decided not to take their backpacks filled with lots of stuff. They only needed a light jacket, a towel, and they would wear their water shoes. Grandma would take care of sunscreen and money in her backpack. They would not take their cameras. They would put their gear in a locker when they knew they would get wet.

The bus ride lasted only fifteen minutes. The theme park was located at 1–10 West and Loop 1604 at exit 555. The closer the kids came to the park, the more excited they got. Grandma reminded Daniel this visit to the theme park was his special request, but she could tell they were all happy about it. This should make for a great afternoon. They would not worry about the rain because they had prepared for it. The rain would only add to their adventure.

The fun started as they bought tickets and walked through the entry pavilion. The anticipation of what was to come caused the excitement for the kids. They laughed and teased each other during lunch. They ordered turkey legs and corn on the cob. They ate holding the turkey leg in one hand and the corn on the cob in the other. Daniel told Grandma they were two-fisted eaters. Ryan said they needed to figure out how to drink without their hands. Anna managed to do just that by drinking out of the straw while the drink rested on the table. The boys tried the same trick, and Daniel reported they were ambidextrous while using their heads. While drinking, Ryan tipped his drink, and it fell over onto the ground. That caused more laughter. When the food was eaten and the ground cleaned up, Grandma led the way to the show "Batman Forever."

"Batman Forever" was great fun. Batman did battle with his archenemies, Two-Face and the Riddler. It was a stunt show featuring high-speed chases and loud explosions. Batman raced around the arena in his Batmobile, and the cast of actors used three groups of cars, motorcycles, and a go-cart to harass each other. It was easy to tell Batman was the hero and Two-Face and The Riddler were the villains. The villains told jokes like, "What can you steal that they won't know you've stolen?" Then Riddler said, "Their minds, silly. We are mind stealers." He called Robin "bird boy" and asked, "What is not right but not wrong?" The answer was the word left. Some of their jokes were funnier than others. No one was safe from them, even the audience.

It had started raining as the family was exiting the arena. The kids were glad they had come prepared for the weather. They then noticed the park had closed down some of the rides as it rained harder. However, the rain made their water rides, Disaster Canyon and Shipwreck Falls, more interesting. Of the two rides, they liked Shipwreck Falls better because of the fifty-foot drop into the splash at the bottom.

Next they went to the Island Kingdom Water Park and put their clothes and jackets and Grandma's backpack into a locker. As they were headed to the Castaway Creek Ride, they couldn't resist getting into the wave pool. They noticed the line was short to Castaway Creek, so they decided now was the time to experience the geysers, water bubbles, and waterfalls. This ride was so fun they went two more times. They would recommend this ride to anyone! It was very wet and a little scary.

The rain let up, and the tourists retrieved their towels from the locker. Grandma sat down on hers to rest while the grandkids headed for the wave pool. They spent the rest of the afternoon jumping waves and waiting for the next wave to come. Hunger pains finally drove them from the pool. They went to the dressing room to put their clothes on for the bus ride to the hotel.

It was getting dark as they stopped for ice cream at the Orchard Café Ice Cream and Subway Parlor and was very dark by the time they exited Six Flags Kids, the gift store with toys, tee shirts, and gifts. The kids bought bright blue tee shirts with a small-embroidered white wave on the front for themselves and then decided the parents should have one too. Ryan made sure he also had one for Brady. Grandma even bought one for herself and Grandpa. They promised they would think of each other when they wore their shirts.

They had to wait for twenty minutes for the shuttle ride to the hotel to arrive. They waited on a bench, and it wasn't until they sat down that they realized how tired they were. They were glad they were headed for the hotel, but Grandma said she was most glad. She felt old and tired and was ready for a break. It was tiring keeping up with kids.

As they were entering the hotel, Gretchen and her brothers, Adam and Jack, were also going in. Gretchen said, "Hi, Anna, we haven't seen you at the pool. How about swimming with us again tonight?"

Forgetting they had just spent the afternoon in the water, Anna turned to her Grandma and said, "Can we?"

After Grandma introduced herself to Gretchen's parents, she said to her grandchildren, "If you guys are up for swimming tonight, that's okay with me. We still have to eat dinner, so what if we say we will meet Gretchen's family at the pool around eight thirty?" Then turning to the parents, Lorraine and Mike, she said, "I will be glad to watch the kids while they swim if you have something else you'd like to do."

Lorraine replied that since this was their last night in San Antonio, it would be nice to take one last walk on the River Walk. They would be glad to accept Grandma's offer.

During dinner Anna said, "Grandma, I didn't think about tonight being our last night in San Antonio until Gretchen's mom mentioned it. Time has gone so quickly. It seems like we just got here, and we go home tomorrow. I can't believe it."

The rest of the group agreed with Anna, and Daniel said, "I can't believe how much has happened to us since we've been here."

Grandma added, "This might be the time to talk about the trip. I'd like to know what each of you thought was the best part and what your answers are to the questions I asked before the trip. What do the words 'the journey makes the destination better' mean to you? And what is the destination, and what is the journey?"

"Grandma, I knew you would ask that question again," said Ryan with a laugh.

"Well, I'm ready to answer it," replied Daniel. "I think we have been on a long journey and we have made many stops. Yes, and those stops are the destinations. So the words mean the better the journey is, the better the destination is."

"So what makes a good journey?" asked Grandma.

"I can answer that," replied Anna. "I think one of the reasons this trip has been so fun is we planned everything out. You let us kids decide some of the things we could do, and that made us feel like it was our trip. Things are always more fun if you have a part in the planning."

"Well I liked that we could change our plan and did change it when we wanted to," was Ryan's input. "Sometimes it is fun not to feel the pressure of a plan."

Grandma answered, "I agree with you all. For me our journey started weeks ago when I first asked you kids to go on this trip. The success and value of this journey to San Antonio has everything to do with you kids and the love we have for each other. When you love someone, everything is better. Love makes you think of other people instead of just thinking about yourself. When you love someone, you are kinder to everyone. We made this trip successful because we all tried hard during the journey. We each did our part because we loved and we took care of each other."

"Yes, and, Anna, all that goes for sisters and brothers too, especially the kind part," added Daniel with a grin on his face.

"You should be so lucky," replied Anna. "I love my little brother, but I reserve the right to smack him if he needs it. That's how you take care of little brothers."

Everyone including Anna laughed at her words. Grandma said, "We all know you love your brother, Anna. Now let's go to the room and get ready for playing in some more water. It's a wonder you kids haven't grown fins or webbed feet."

"What about our answers to the rest of your questions?" asked Ryan.

"You can answer what you liked best about the destinations and the journey later," answered Grandma. "We have been serious long enough. I want to remind you to obey the rules for the hotel swimming pool. They are the same as the first night, or should I say the last time you went swimming at this hotel. Here's one for you. How can the first be the last?"

Anna answered, "Grandma, I thought you said we'd been serious long enough."

"It was a joke, Anna, get it? The last time you went swimming was the first time? Oh well, I've never been good with jokes," replied Grandma. Grandma didn't say it, but she couldn't wait until the next hour of this journey was over and the kids were all showered and tucked into bed. She was tired. She thought,

Grandpa, where are you when I need you? The late-night swimming encouraged the needed relaxation, and this day's journey ended with a snoring chorus of sleep.

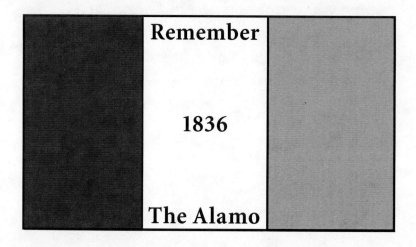

Remember

1836

The Alamo

Will you Remember the Alamo?

Grandma awakened the next morning feeling refreshed and ready for the last day of Destination: San Antonio. As she lay in bed listening to her grandchildren sleep, she reflected upon the joy of grandchildren and the give and take of this unique relationship. She believed for every effort she put into the relationship, she received much more. She and Grandpa had worked to create a bond with the kids, even when it was sometimes inconvenient and tiring. These children and their parents were the legacy they would leave to this world. Nothing could be more important than these relationships for developing secure, self-confident, creative adults who could make wise choices and who were willing to give back to God and country. As a grandma and grandpa, they had been investing in the future of this family and would continue to do so all of their days. Now it was time to get on with the day. Grandma whispered, "Bring it on. I'm ready."

She awakened the kids with a kiss on their heads. She knew this would not embarrass them because they were too sleepy to care. All her sentimental reflections of the morning should be worth something. Anna woke up immediately, but it took Daniel and Ryan longer. Grandma said, "Rise and shine and give God the glory."

Daniel said, "Grandma, I know your mom got you up in the morning with those words and you got my mom up with them, but I just don't see any glory in getting up in the morning. Give me a few minutes, and I will come around."

Ryan added, "I'm the same way."

"Okay, kids," Grandma replied, "but for the sake of time, you should be able to listen while you are lying in your bed. We need to check out of this hotel by 11:00 a.m. Do you remember we thought we'd go back to the Alamo this morning? I'm not sure we could be back before checkout time, so we need to pack and take our bags with us before we head to the Alamo. It dawned on me we hadn't taken any pictures of it, so we need to be sure to take our cameras. I know we don't need a picture to create a memory, but pictures will help us to remember this trip after several months go by. Next, it seems like a good plan to pack, then to eat breakfast here in the hotel, and then to check out. The hotel has a room where we can keep our luggage until we leave for the airport at 1:00 p.m. Does that sound okay with you?"

By now the kids were sitting up in their beds. Anna said, "Sure, I think I'm getting excited to go home. I miss my parents and my things. It won't take me long to pack because most of my clothes are dirty. I'll just stuff them in my laundry bag and put it in my suitcase."

Grandma answered her with, "That shows good planning, Anna. You packed efficiently if you don't have clothes that you didn't wear. What about you, boys?"

Ryan said, "If dirty clothes show efficiency, I'm very efficient. All my clothes are dirty, but I do have clean underwear left. Guess I'll wear the same clothes home that I came in. That will freak my mom out. When she sees me, she will think I wore the same clothes all weekend."

Daniel said, "That's cool. All my shirts are dirty, but I do have one pair of clean jeans. Maybe I'll wear my dirty stuff so I can bug my mom."

"I don't think it will matter to your moms what you wear home. They will be so glad to see you they won't care what you look like. They have missed you so much they are probably waiting for you at the airport right now," added Grandma.

"Okay, okay, yes, I'm getting excited now," said Daniel. "Let's get going with our day. First person finished packing is the winner."

"Remember to check the bathroom for things you might have left in there. It's very easy to leave toothpaste or shampoo," reminded Grandma.

It did not take long for the kids and grandma to be dressed and packed. They straightened up and checked the room one more time to see if they had left anything. They were ready. They were ready to eat, to see the Alamo, but most of all they all were ready to go home. With this focus, the tasks were soon completed, and the family hit the River Walk with full bellies.

This time as they entered the Alamo, they took time to read the signs. They read that the people of Texas believed this building was a shrine to those who had died defending the Alamo. It was a sacred place and would be treated accordingly. Hats had to be removed before entering, and voices must be respectful and subdued.

Grandma whispered, "Let's take a tour and see if the guide agrees with what you experienced here. Let's see if they have their history straight."

"That's a great idea, Grandma. I think our

trip back in time made us experts, so let's check it out," agreed Daniel.

The family joined a group standing with a guide. She said, "Good morning, I am Docent Lois. Since 1905 the Texas State Legislature has entrusted the Daughters of the Republic of Texas with the care and maintenance of the Alamo. According to Texas, the DRT, that's us, must preserve the historic site 'as a sacred memorial to the heroes who immolated themselves upon that hallowed ground.' With no monetary help from the local, state, or federal government, we depend solely on the money from donations and proceeds from the gift shop to preserve the complex and to maintain exhibits. We are open Monday through Saturday from 9:00 a.m. to 5:30 p.m. and on Sundays from 10:00 a.m. to 5:30 p.m. The Alamo complex is open every day of the year except Christmas Eve and Christmas Day. Admission is free.

Before we begin this tour, I wish to take you back in history to December 26, 1835, when Daniel Cloud *en route* to San Antonio De Bexar said, and I quote, 'If we succeed the Country is ours. It is immense in extent, and fertile in its soil and will amply reward all our toil. If we fail, death in the cause of liberty and humanity is not cause for shuddering. Our rifles are by our side, and choice guns they are, we know what awaits us, and are prepared to meet it. Daniel William Cloud was from Kentucky, and he died here in the Battle for the Alamo."

Her small group followed as Docent Lois continued, "The Battle for the Alamo was decisive in the war for an independent Texas because it was a place where men made the ultimate sacrifice for freedom. Men died here so others might govern themselves. Men died here fighting against overwhelming odds. Around two hundred volunteers under Colonel William B. Travis fought bravely against thousands of Mexican *soldados* under Mexican General Antonio Lopez de Santa Anna for thirteen days. The final assault came before daybreak on the morning of March 6, 1836. All the defenders died except the women and children and slaves. To further humiliate the defenders, Santa Anna ordered a funeral pyre built with the soldiers' bodies. To build the pyre, they placed a layer of bodies and then a layer of wood and then another layer of bodies until the pile rose high. The bodies of these heroes were then burned, and the fire could be seen for miles. That act was so repugnant it has gone down in history with the rallying cry, 'Remember the Alamo.' That cry motivated the drive to be rid of the hated Santa Anna and to avenge the massacre at the Alamo. The defenders of the Alamo lost the battle but helped to win the war for independence. Now if you will follow me, the tour will continue in the next room."

Grandma and the kids decided not to follow. They were totally caught up in the drama again. There were important things they needed to talk about. Grandma said, "I remember seeing a picnic table in the park outside the gift shop. Let's go there, and we will be free to talk. Afterwards we can see what the gift shop has to offer."

Sitting at the picnic table gave the family some privacy. They could take as many pictures as they wanted, and this would be the best place for the kids to finish answering Grandma's questions about the trip and to experience their trip back in time once more.

"I remember that Señora Esparza was still cleaning up after the evening meal when we arrived," said Anna. "The women had taken the meals to the defenders while they were firing the long rifles and cannons. The defenders had hardly stopped to eat. Even I could see there wasn't much food left for the next day. Señora Esparza said they had already killed all the cows and chickens the men had brought inside the Alamo compound for food so there would no longer be milk or eggs to eat. Señora Esparza told me she was worried about what to do when it was all gone."

"I remember that Señor Esparza said the ammunition was running low, too," added Daniel. "You can't fight a war without ammunition."

"I remember how tired everyone was," said Ryan. "No one was getting much sleep because of that awful song. I can't remember what the Mexicans called it."

"It was called a *degüello,*" answered Anna. "That song was so creepy; no wonder the defenders couldn't sleep."

"Then I guess Santa Anna was pretty smart

with his strategies. If he wanted to weaken his enemy, he sure accomplished that," said Grandma. "Wars are about leadership and strategies. You win some and you lose some."

"Santa Anna was a very bad guy," said Daniel.

"I think it's hard to tell the good guys from the bad guys in war," replied Grandma. "I think the good guys are on your side, and the bad guys are on the other side. It depends which side you are on because the guys we think are the bad guys think we are the bad guys. We can't say the winners are the good guys because as we learned from the Battle of the Alamo, the good guys lost. War gets very confusing."

"Maybe the meanest bad guys win," continued Daniel. "Burning the defenders' bodies was the worst. And remember Santa Anna didn't care how many of his *soldados* had to die. Yes, he was the baddest of the bad."

Grandma laughed at his remark and said, "Well, Daniel, I don't know if *baddest* is a word, but it sure fits here. Not to change the subject, but what do the good guys, that's us, think was the best part of our trip to San Antonio, Texas?"

"I think it was all good, Grandma," answered Ryan. "I liked it all."

"I'm glad," answered Grandma. "Tell me why you think that."

"You're making us think," said Anna. "It's easier to say what Ryan said than to make a choice."

"I think I liked our trip back in time the best because no one else that I know has done that. In my whole life I will never forget Enrique and David Crockett," answered Daniel.

"I think I liked our trip back in time the best because I have never been so scared in my life," added Ryan. "I thought I was going to die for sure when those *soldados* pointed their guns at us, and then of course there was Jim Bowie's knife. I'm not about to forget about that."

"Well, Grandma, I liked our trip back in time the best too," continued Anna. "I liked it the best because we found out how to go back in time. I plan to do it again."

"Oh my, Anna, that's risky," answered her Grandma. "Please promise me you will check with your parents before you do that."

"Okay, that's an easy promise to make,"

answered Anna. "It's like letting your parents know your plans. It goes back to the trust thing. Besides that's a family rule. Parents need to know where you are at all times. What's your favorite thing, Grandma? It's your turn to tell."

"I think my favorite part of this trip was watching you kids enjoy yourselves," answered Grandma. "I just liked being with you. After this trip I wouldn't be afraid to take you anywhere. You were cooperative and kind to one another. You obeyed when I asked you to do something, and you didn't whine and complain when things did not go your way. You were enthusiastic and excited. Those things are very important to me. There's only one thing I'm sorry about, and that is Brady. I wish he'd been old enough to come with us. As soon as possible, we need to take another trip so he can come. I've been thinking about a trip to California or Florida. Maybe I will let you guys decide where we will go next time. We'll see. Now let's go check out the gift shop before it's time to head back to the hotel to pick up our luggage and catch the shuttle to the airport. We want to get to the airport in plenty of time so we don't have to be stressed. Ready?"

Grandma only had to say those words one time. The kids practically raced through the gift shop. Daniel and Ryan bought fake knives, Anna bought a gold cat's-eye ring, and Grandma bought three little flags. She refused to let the grandkids look at them. She also bought a car for Brady. She let the kids see that.

It was later than they thought when the family arrived at the hotel. The boys quickly put the knives into their suitcases so there would be no trouble going through security at the airport; they went to the bathroom and then boarded the shuttle. They were excited as they anticipated the flight home, but this time it was different. Anna and Daniel felt like seasoned travelers. They had been there and done that. Traveling on an airplane had been a piece of cake. It was nothing they couldn't handle. When compared to time travel, three hours was nothing. Besides, their mom and maybe their dad would be waiting at the gate. Anna and Daniel couldn't wait to see them.

Grandma was a little sad as she watched the

kids eat their lunch. It seemed as if it had been days ago since they had first arrived and had eaten their first meal together in this very food court. Now it was time to continue their journey home. They had checked in and gone through security without a hitch. Grandma would be going back to Georgia with Ryan so she could spend some time with Brady. Then she would go home to Grandpa. Maybe Grandpa could come on the next trip. Time would tell.

Ryan and Grandma walked Anna and Daniel to their gate, where the attendant waited to escort then onto the plane. As Grandma kissed and hugged the kids good-bye, she handed them each a flag with the instructions not to read what was written on it until they were on the airplane. Ryan would get his flag when he boarded his airplane. Anna and Daniel couldn't wait to look, and as they walked down the jet way to the airplane they looked. In bright red letters was written "Remember the Alamo!"

The End

Glossary of Spanish Words

1. acequia–Water channel that runs through a village
2. agua–Water
3. Alamo–Poplar tree
4. baño–Bathroom
5. Canary Is.–From Spanish Islas Canarias, where the canary birds are from
6. Coahuila–Northern state of Mexico of which Texas was a part
7. Feliz Navidad–Merry Christmas
8. gato–Cat
9. degüello–Battle cry for take no prisoners
10. escopeta–Musket
11. hermana–Sister
12. hermano–Brother
13. LA Los Angeles–originally Our Lady of the Angels in Spanish
14. La Villita–The little village
15. mamá–Mother
16. Mercado–Market
17. papá–Father

18. Paso del Río–Where the
    river flows or river pass
19. perro–Dog
20. piñata–A papier-mâché figure broken
    by children taking turns hitting it
21. Río Loco–Crazy River
22. San Antonio–Saint Anthony
23. sombrero–Hat
24. señor–Title for sir or mister
25. señora–Title for madam or missus
26. soldado–Soldier
27. Tejanos–Hispanic people born in Texas
28. Texas–From Spanish *Tejas*.
    Originally a Native American term
    for the group of inhabitants liv-
    ing there when the Spanish arrived.
    It means friend or friendly.

Discussion Questions for Each Chapter Using Bloom's Taxonomy

* Please note: There is a discussion question for each chapter.

The numbers of the questions match the numbers of the chapters.

These questions were developed using *Bloom's Taxonomy of Cognitive Process.*

1. Knowledge: Describe the relationship between Anna and Daniel.
2. Comprehension: Discuss the time zones in the United States. Discuss their purpose. Do you think they are necessary? Include daylight savings time.
3. Comprehension: When the new girl enters her sixth-grade classroom, she sees a banner saying, "Sixth-grade Rules: Be a Role Model." Do you agree or disagree with the banner? Explain your reasons.
4. Application: How would you solve the hazard of the escaping steam from the popcorn cooked in the microwave?

5. Analysis: Anna and Daniel's family set rules for using their family computer. Does your family have rules concerning the use of a computer? Compare your rules to the rules listed in the book. Are yours more efficient? Why or why not?

6. Synthesis: Ryan and Brady are brothers. Brady is much younger and wants to be able to do everything Ryan does. Discuss your feelings in relation to siblings, age, and activities. Do you believe everything should be equal? Why or why not?

7. Evaluation: The grandkids play organized sports. Some kids decide to opt out. Discuss the pros and cons of playing organized sports as a kid. How would you have handled the dad who coached from the sidelines and yelled at his son?

8. Knowledge: Ryan and his friends Aaron and Tommy have rules for after school. They can get into real trouble if they disobey them. Do you have after-school rules? Describe them. Do you think they are fair? Describe what would happen in your family when your parents don't know where you are.

9. Synthesis: Grandma created an umbrella plan as a guide for the trip. Pretend you are going with the family to San Antonio. How would you improve the Umbrella Plan?

10. Knowledge: Grandma sent "The Parable of Wasted Time" to her grandkids. What was the meaning of the story, and why did she send it?

11. Knowledge: On the flight to San Antonio, Anna reads abut Amelia Earhart. Why was she an important person is history? Who is your favorite historical person and why?

12. Knowledge: Tell about a time a suspicious person scared you. How did you handle it? What would you do differently?

13. Comprehension: Explain how using a map of Sea World helped Grandma and the kids enjoy the experience.

14. Comprehension: When making a decision in a group, the decisions of a majority of the people in the group usually prevail. Explain why those decisions can be both good and bad.

15. Synthesis: Imagine you were a defender of the Alamo. What could you do to improve your chances for survival? If everyone had survived would the outcome have been different? How and why?

16. Knowledge: Name some reasons why people fight wars. Who are the good guys, and who are the bad guys? Why do you think so?

17. Comprehension: The Cousins received a standing ovation for their performance at the Arneson Theatre. Why do you think that happened? If you decided to play an instrument which one would it be?

18. Evaluation: The grandkids spoke Enrique's Spanish language when they met him in the acequia. Judge the value of being able to speak the language of the person you are communicating with.

19. Synthesis: Predict what Grandma would've done if the grandkids had insisted all of them should travel back in time to the Alamo the next day. Would

she have gone? Why or why not? Would you have gone?

20. Comprehension: Explain the words "Remember the Alamo!"

Internet Sites for Maps

1. http://infoplease.com/atlas/state/texas. html–Texas Atlas; Maps and Online Resources
2. http://www.traveltex.com/TexasMap. aspx–Texas Interactive Map
3. http://www.thesanantonioriverwalk. com/maps/index.asp–free maps of the River Walk in San Antonio
4. http://www.sanantonio.com/airport/ index.html–airport information
5. http://seaworld.com/sanantonio–see video
6. http://www.seaworld.com/sitePage. aspx?Page1D=60–directions to Sea World
7. http://www.thealamo.org/visitors. html–information about the Alamo
8. http://www.sixflags.com/parks/ fiestatexas/index.asp–video, information about Six Flags Fiesta Texas

e|LIVE

listen|imagine|view|experience